ABOUT THE A

Peter Downey has both bachelor and masters degrees but he doesn't often like to let on that he is also a doctor because his doctoral study was, in fact, in *education* not *medicine*, and he is afraid that on a long-haul flight over the Pacific a flight attendant will ask 'Is there a doctor on board' and he will put his hand up and then have to go to the back of the plane and deliver a baby despite trying to explain the mistake but no one will listen to him because of the woman's screams and it will only be after he has conducted a caesarean with nothing but airline cutlery and a plastic sewing kit that the confusion will be explained and he will be labelled 'Airline Hero' in his local newspaper.

Downey already has two internationally successful parenting books under his belt, both known for their down-to-earth, humorous style.

However, his main qualification for writing a book about marriage lies in the fact that he is (in his own words) an 'extra-ordinarily average' red-brick-house-in-the-suburbs kind of guy who has been ludicrously happily married with children for more than ten years.

By the way, he publicly apologises for the mullet haircut he had on his wedding day (see photo, this page). But it was fashionable at the time.

Honest.

Everything a BLOKE needs to know about MARRIAGE

Peter Downey

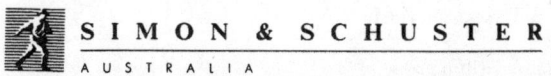
SIMON & SCHUSTER
AUSTRALIA

EVERYTHING A BLOKE NEEDS TO KNOW ABOUT MARRIAGE
First published in Australia in 2000 by
Simon & Schuster (Australia) Pty Limited
20 Barcoo Street, East Roseville NSW 2069

A Viacom Company
Sydney New York London Toronto Tokyo Singapore

© Peter Downey 2000

All rights reserved. No part of this publication may be reproduced, stored in a retrieval system, or transmitted, in any form or by any means, electronic, mechanical, photocopying, recording or otherwise, without the prior permission of the publisher in writing.

National Library of Australia
Cataloguing-in-Publication data

Downey, Peter, 1964 – .
  Everything a bloke needs to know about marriage.

  Bibliography.
  ISBN 0 7318 0952 1.

  1. Marriage. 2. Marriage – Humor. 3. Husbands. 4. Husband and wife. 5. Man–woman relationships. I. Title.

306.81

The FJ Holden pictured on the front cover is courtesy of FJ Holden Wedding Cars, 37 Smith St, Wentworthville, NSW 2145. Tel: (02) 9636 2005.

Design by Gayna Murphy, Greendot Design
Cartoons by Nik Scott
Typesetting by Asset Typesetting Pty Ltd
Set in 11/14 Sabon
Printed in Australia by Griffin Press

10 9 8 7 6 5 4 3 2 1

This book is dedicated to my wife, Meredith J. Downey: girlfriend at age 16, wife at 21, best friend ever since.

[A married man] will, in a general way, become sordid, and thrifty, and domesticated; he will learn to glory more in buying articles cheap at sales than in carrying off trophies from his compeers; he will become particular over his tucker, and cautious about getting his feet wet; he will become prudent and circumspect, and churchwardenlike, and befittingly frightened in the presence of anything lawless, from a crash of thunder to a scrub-bred steer ...

TOM COLLINS,
THE BULN-BULN AND THE BROLGA

(c. 1905; posthumous publication 1948)

I do ...

PETER DOWNEY,
10 DECEMBER (11 YEARS AGO)

Contents

Acknowledgements xi
Preface xiii
Prologue: Marriage? You must be kidding! xviii

Part One: Getting Married

1 Contemplation (should we or shouldn't we?) 3
   Marriage: What is it? 4
   Marriage: Why would you? 10

2 Engagement (the fun bit) 17
   Popping the question 18
   Going public 24
   So, you're engaged 29
   Learning the ropes 33

3. Preparations (the spin-out) 37
   Get involved 38
   I thought this was *my* wedding 42
   Learning to negotiate 47
   Ker-ching! Ker-ching! 50
   The vortex 55
   What's in a name? 59
   But it's tradition... 62

4. Practicalities (someone has to organise it) 67
   Timing, timing... 68
   Guest list 75
   Invitations 82
   What to Wear? 88
   Music 91
   Watch the birdie 98
   'I do': the most important bit 103

5. Let's Celebrate (letting your hair down) 113
   Reception basics 114
   Reception traditions 120
   Organising the honeymoon 133

6. The Big Day (this is it) 137
Buck's night 138
On the day 144
Scrub up 148
Murphy's Wedding 152
That first night 156

Part Two: Staying Married

7. Happily ever after (you hope...) 163
The carnival is over 164
Settling in 167
Eye to eye 1: Not getting on 170
Eye to eye 2: Working it out 179
Honey, I bought you some roses... 187
Keep it in your daks 197
The best things in life are free 207
The in-laws 214
Cleaning the oven 218
525 600 minutes 223
The patter of little feet 227
Get Real! 231
Happily ever after 235

Epilogue: Throwim Way Leg 239

THE STUFF AT THE BACK 243
What my mates had to say 244
Films 258
Glossary 266
References 276
Peter Downey launches into cyberspace 279
Gratuitous self-promotion page 281

Acknowledgements

Thanks to:

- Meredith, my wife and voice of reason. The fact that I'm writing a book about marriage is a tribute to you. Thank you for your commitment, love, support, tolerance, proofreading, 'time at the keyboard' and for laughing at my jokes, even when they're not funny.

    If only you could learn to pour a beer without frothing it all up over the side of the glass and all over the bench-top, you'd be perfect.

    Is that too much to ask?

    Is it?

    And while I'm at it, keep your icy feet off me in the middle of the night... it's like being in bed with an iceberg... grumble ... mumble...

    Seriously, thanks for the best years of my life. You are a jewel in the Ethiop's ear.
- My children, Rachael, Georgia and Matilda, for understanding when they came out to my study to tell me something really important that happened at school that day... and I told them to buzz off cos I was writing a book.

- My parents, Hilda and Stan, for teaching me about service, tolerance, contentment and Saturday-morning omelettes.
- All the gang at Simon and Schuster: associate publisher Julie Stanton for signing me up, barely-managing editor Brigitta Doyle for advice about guinea pigs, editor Susan Gray for putting red lines through most of my original manuscript, and my publicist, Fiona Robinson, who hasn't done anything yet, but who no doubt will get me lots of great TV, radio and press coverage and hopefully a trip to Paris.
- All and sundry wedding professionals who sent me brochures and chatted to me on the phone. You know how I said I was getting married? I lied.
- All my married mates, who have educated and enlightened me about marriage. Thank you for all your emails, stories, comments, advice and beers. By the way, Nigel, I think you have to spend a bit more time on foreplay.

Preface

All tragedies are finish'd by a death
All comedies are ended by a marriage

LORD BYRON

I put my arm around my wife, Meredith, and stared contentedly into her eyes. She smiled at me and we kissed. With a deep breath, I reflected for a moment on how successful my marriage was.

Married life was fantastic. Sure, I'd had a few anxieties at first, but they soon disappeared and everything was as they had said it would be ... and more.

Then again, I had only been married for 16 minutes, so I was hardly what you would call an expert.

I met Meredith when I was eighteen.

She was, in truth, the little sister of my then-girlfriend (a fact that still carries a residue of awkwardness at family gatherings). There were no lightning-bolts of love, and I didn't really notice her at the time, apart from the fact that her long hair cascaded like honey gossamer down her shoulders framing her angelic face with its piercing green eyes and moist pouting lips, and the way her swimming costume tightly hugged her curvaceous and fulsome ... oh, sorry, where was I?

I'd had plenty of girlfriends before, nearly all of whom dumped me. (Hello girls, look who's laughing now. I have a doctorate and three books published, a beautiful wife, three great kids, a red-brick house in a leafy suburb and a very expensive Tarago. By the way, Catherine, I hear you and Paul aren't together anymore. Too bad. He's seeing someone else, isn't he? That's what I heard. Pity you dumped me for him. Because I really think commitment is important. But no hard feelings. Really.)

I won't bore you with the details, especially not about the night we first kissed while watching *The Elephant Man*. You only need to know that we 'went around' together for a few years before getting married on the hottest summer's day in recorded history. I was 24 and she was twenty-one.

And here I am, looking back on 11 years of earth-shatteringly good marriage, writing a book to tell you everything a bloke needs to know about marriage. Look at it as a 'been there, done that, here's how I survived' thing.

Between you and me, writing a book about weddings and marriage was not quite as simple or straightforward as I first envisaged.

Attitudes and rituals relating to the joining of a man and a woman in marriage reflect the specific time and the specific culture, and even sub-culture, in which they live. Marriage is such a complex, varied and changing part of our culture that in trying to make sense of the whole wedding/marriage circus, any book on the topic will be filled with broad generalisations, cultural assumptions, sweeping statements, moral judgements and editorial exclusions.

And so, this book is an amalgam of my own moral values and attitudes, modified by conversations and sketchy research, combined with email humour and magazine reading, interwoven with years of observation of (and participation in) numerous weddings, and loosely drawn together by inspirational ideas that came to me at 3 am. It reflects my middle-class white Anglo-Saxon western-world traditional suburban surf-culture semi-conservative family-values university-educated middle-

Preface

management meat-and-three-veg Christian attitudes, experiences, background and upbringing.

So if you're a Fuhngizi tribesman looking for how many goats to trade for a bride, you're looking in the wrong place.

But if you're a suburban bloke wanting to know how to word a wedding invitation or what to do when you and your wife have an argument over who left a tissue in their pocket before it went into the washing machine, this is the book for you.

This is the third book I've written, not counting my disaster novel about a passenger submarine and an iceberg. (It truly was a disaster, but what do you expect? I was only sixteen.) It's a book in two parts. The first part is about preparing for that enormous logistical nightmare — your wedding day. The second part deals with the oft-forgotten but far more important part — namely, the years of marriage that follow.

I wrote this book because:

- I needed something to keep my typing fingers busy while waiting for my children to grow into teenagers so I can write the final saga in my parenting trilogy. Also, when not typing, I moped around the house and bothered my wife for sex and she got sick of me.
  So I was exiled to the study.
  And after I high-scored computer pinball, I needed something else to amuse me.
- I need the money. I'm still trying to get together a deposit for a villa in Portugal, but a new Tarago and a propensity towards imported lagers have devastated my bank account.
- I believe in marriage. (*Trumpet fanfare, maestro ...*)

I think that the formal, long-term and monogamous commitment of one man and one woman is, in relationship terms, a jolly good idea. It's been around for thousands of years, in various forms, and along with several other billion people in the world, I think marriage is terrific. I want you to enjoy being

xv

married as much as I do, although this is unlikely because I've got the best wife in the world and any woman you snare will not be as good as mine, so bad luck, fella.

I'm an old-fashioned guy. I believe in family and marriage and commitment and love and all that other stuff, even in these bleak days where newspapers scream that 'marriage is dead'.

Part of this obviously comes from the fact that I really enjoy my own marriage. I love the sense of belonging, intimacy, friendship, closeness and companionship I share with my wife. I like it that she knows me better than anyone else and that, God willing, we will grow old together. A good marriage can be rewarding, fulfilling and exciting. That's to say nothing of the astoundingly great sex ... which I'm not going to go into right now, because, quite frankly, it's none of your business.

But there's a lot of misconceptions about marriage. On TV it's portrayed as a perfect harmonious match (aka 'The Brady Bunch'), a hilarious romantic romp (aka 'The Nanny'), a soppy domestic adventure (aka 'Seventh Heaven') or a miserable and pathetic nightmare (aka 'Married with Children').

Marriage is hard work. Don't let anyone tell you otherwise. When you cut through the stereotypes, marriage is about long-term, heavy-duty, difficult-at-times and just plain unromantic commitment. It's about sharing, companionship, responsibility, sacrifice and service. It's about waking up next to the same woman every morning, not in sexy lingerie in a room of billowing white curtains, but rather in flannelette pyjamas with facial pillow creases and bad breath.

Yes, your wedding day is a 'very special day'. And yes, your marriage should be full of joy and wonder and love and warmth and understanding and sharing and fun and companionship. But all that romantic stuff is only half the story.

This book is a whirlwind tour through the marriage experience, from popping the question through to surviving your first year as a married man. It is not an in-depth academic exploration as much as a fly-by. The chapters are brief and shallow (reflecting my personality), and if you want to read more about conflict resolution or domestic financial management or communication skills or rekindling passion in your marriage, or if you want to get one of those wedding planner/checklist books, then go to the bookshop and choose from any one of a squillion thick tomes. This is not the book for you.

It is my genuine and simple hope that this book will open your eyes to a few ideas, make you stop and think about something you haven't thought of before, help to clarify a few issues, suggest something innovative for your wedding day ... and maybe, just maybe, improve the chances that you will grow gracefully old with your wife in a long and deeply satisfying marriage.

And if it stops you from wearing a brown velour suit on your wedding day, then it's all been worthwhile.

So turn the page and let's check out everything a bloke needs to know about marriage.

Prologue: Marriage? You must be kidding!

> *For in what stupid age or nation*
> *Was marriage ever out of fashion?*
>
> SAMUEL BUTLER

I told a friend that I was writing a book on weddings and marriage. She was surprised.

'Marriage?' said she, 'That's on the way out. A thing of the past. Most people just live together these days. Don't waste your time.'

I only had a split second to come up with a witty rebuff:

'You're only saying that as a defence mechanism because you're physically repulsive, have no sense of humour and no-one will ever marry you.'

(Okay, so I don't respond well to criticism.)

But she raised an interesting point, one worthy of our consideration at this early stage. The union of man and woman, whether formalised as *marriage* or not, has been the mainstay of civilisation across all cultures since the beginning of time.

This is because, in a nutshell, humans are relational beings, and despite all our prattlings about freedom and individuality, and despite the detritus of the sexual revolution, at the end of the day we all want someone to love us, listen to us and snuggle up to on a cold night.

Back in the days of primordial sludge, there were no rings, engagement parties or promises to love and honour. You simply dragged your woman into the cave by her hair and used a yak thighbone to beat the crap out of anyone who came near her.

Fortunately for the woman (and the yak), those days have long gone. 'Marriage' has changed.

We are living now in a groovy, post-modern, retro-funk era of rapidly changing information technology where individuality is king and redefinition and uncertainty are the very stuff of life itself. Life zooms by in a flurry of emails, takeaway pizzas and mobile phone conversations, interspersed with late-night coffees and early-morning squash games. We live in a world of disposable bags, disposable pens, disposable razors, disposable nappies and disposable marriages.

The point is, many people hold a sense of pessimism about the ability of marriage 'to deliver' in today's world.

People are more socially and financially independent, and couples are more flexible, tending not to waltz into permanence. Many couples live de facto and they are more cautious about marriage, with 62% of men and 55% of women believing that a trial marriage is a good idea, and 80% of couples stating that it's okay for couples to live together without planning to get married.

So, more than half the total number of couples live together first before they get married — which, by the bye, usually occurs later (the median age for first marriage has risen to 28, up by five years on the last generation). Some couples choose to draw up complicated legal documents and pre-nuptial agreements. Even then, odds are that a good percentage will be in the divorce court before the honeymoon snaps have even been developed, with a current divorce rate of 40% (which is 25% up on ten years ago). Sadly, 8% of couples won't even get to their fifth wedding anniversary. Sunday papers scream that marriage is dead, that it's a romantic anachronism and that the clouds are gathering over a brief golden age of euphoria about marriage. One UK mag even came up with a 'Ditch your loser with a free divorce' headline and a $1000 prize for the best breakdown story, while an Australian company now offers a DIY divorce kit over the net.

Sounds pretty bleak, doesn't it?

Strangely and paradoxically, though, marriage is booming and weddings are big business. Last year, the number of marriages actually *increased* for the first time in 20 years.

Half of all couples living de facto will eventually walk down the aisle. And while divorce rates are going through the roof, so too are rates of re-marriage. Last year, 35% of people getting married were up for their second go. Reception venues are booked for months or even years in advance. Brides' dresses are still white and expensive and elaborate. There are more bridal magazines on the stands than ever before. Every weekend, classic cars with white ribbons cram our roads, while our parks and beaches are crowded with bridal parties having glamour photo shoots in front of burning ochre sunsets. Romantic resorts are besieged by ecstatic newlyweds with shiny gold wedding bands and his'n'hers T-shirts.

Despite all the doom and gloom, people still love a good wedding. Women's magazines remain fixated with cover stories of celebrity weddings. Marriage, it seems, is still culturally and emotionally in vogue. (In fact, surveys show that marriage is regarded as a critical ingredient to a satisfying life and is still the most widely desired lifestyle choice. A recent *Relationships Australia* survey revealed that people aged 18 to 24 are still highly committed to the concept of relationships and that marriage is still viewed by them as a lifelong commitment. Social researcher Hugh Mackay also claims that young people still cling on to the expectations that they will one day marry and have children.)

Besides all this (and purely and selfishly from the male point of view), married guys have a lower incidence of heart disease, longer life expectancy, lower incidence of cancer, decreased suicide rate, 50% more regular sex and $200 more in their weekly pay packet than their single buddies. They also put on more weight, because the food is better. It's all rather confusing.

So where does that leave you, poised as you are on the brink of your marital journey? Where do you fit into this maelstrom of shifting social practice and conflicting messages?

In no-man's-land, that's where. Stuck in the marital twilight zone between 'Marriage is an archaic and dying institution' and 'Should we have four tiers on the cake, or five?'. But ultimately it doesn't matter what the papers and the sociologists and the census say. It doesn't matter what the trends are or what the statistics imply. You're a big boy. Make up your own mind.

The only thing that matters is your relationship with the woman you love. Sure, there are people who don't get married. Sure, a lot of marriages don't work. But so what? Ask yourself the hard questions:

Do you want to spend the rest of your life with her or not?

Do you want to grow old together and see her as the mother of your children?

Will you take her and remain committed and faithful to her no matter what happens?

Can she cook better than you?

Is she a good companion?

Can you see yourself without her?

Can you resolve your disputes and work through the hard times?

Oh, and can you cope with the fact that she's going to end up just like her mother?

Just remember this: after the exhausting circus of your wedding day is over, after the photographer has left and the guests have gone home and the music has died, after you've cut the cake and made the speeches and kissed everybody in sight and got a cramp in your face from smiling, after you've driven off into the sunset and shut the door behind you, you're together. And like they say in the hokey-pokey, *that's what it's all about.*

You.

Her.

Married.

After all the fuss is over, it all boils down to one thing: companionship. The two of you, just hanging out together, waking up next to each other, watching telly, talking about stuff, having a coffee, making plans for your future, having great holidays, laughing, arguing over stupid things, growing old…

Oh, and there's also the whole sex thing.

Part One
Getting Married

1
Contemplation
(should we or shouldn't we?)

'I always knew I'd get married eventually, but it wasn't quite as simple as I thought. You know, no-one's exactly jumping into marriage like they used to. There's lots of divorce, and most of our friends live together. We used to say, a marriage certificate is just a piece of paper.

But after eight months of living together, we knew it was for life, so we got married.

Deb has an Economics degree hanging on our wall. The paper itself doesn't make her an accountant. But it represents the fact that she studied and is qualified to do the job.

In the same way, our marriage certificate doesn't keep us together as if it's magic. It is still just a piece of paper. But it does signify something bigger: our love and commitment to each other.'

STEVE, 32

Marriage: What is it?

> *Marriage is obsolete: a trap for both sexes where the man becomes a boss and the woman becomes a shrew.*
>
> CATHERINE DENEUVE

Before you go leaping off down the aisle in a rented tux, let's first look at what you're thinking of getting into.

What is marriage?

Let's, for a moment, cut the crap about bridal waltzes, glamour photography and cans dragged behind the car. Marriage is a formal arrangement and a matter of law. It is a legal process with legal consequences and responsibilities. My *Macquarie Dictionary* defines marriage as:

> the legal or religious ceremony that sanctions or formalises the decision of a man and woman to live as husband and wife.

When you marry the woman of your dreams, you enter into a legal contract. You make a formal and public declaration of your love and commitment to her as you join together to form a new social and economic family unit.

There are a number of rules and regulations about this:

- You can only be married to one woman at a time. She may be single or divorced or widowed, but neither of you can be currently married. If you have multiple wives, you can get into a lot of trouble for bigamy. Just ask Giovanni Vigliotto and any one of his 104 wives. But at least you can cover your legal fees by appearing on a current affairs show or in a women's magazine.
- Marriage must be entered into *voluntarily*. If you get married because your pregnant girlfriend's dad posted you a shotgun shell with your name etched into the casing, then it's not legally binding.
- Marriage must be entered into with the understanding that it is for life. While everyone knows about the high divorce rates, you can't get married with the intention of it being a temporary measure. It is not the kind of thing you would do to fill in a dull summer holiday, for example.
- One of you should be a woman and one should be a man.
- You have to give adequate official notice to the government of your intention to marry. Generally, this is done by filling in the very appropriately titled 'Notice of Intended Marriage' form and submitting it at least one month and one day before your wedding.
- You cannot marry anyone genealogically close to you in your family tree. The 1961 Commonwealth Marriage Act forbids marriage between you and:
  — any of your ancestors (Mum, Grandma, Great Grandma)
  — any of your descendants (daughter, grand-daughter)
  — any of your sisters.

These include full-blood, half-blood and adopted relatives. I know it must be a great disappointment to you that Grannie is off your list, but it's for the best. All you have to do is look at royal families throughout history to discern a certain inbred madness in the bloodlines. That's to say nothing of banjo players.

- You have to be of the appropriate legal age, as prescribed by the law of your country or area. In Bangladesh in 1986, a three-month-old girl was married to an 11-month-old boy. They had a reception where they feasted on mushy carrots and breast milk, before their honeymoon in a cot at the bride's parents' house. Most Western countries, however, have a higher minimum age, generally eighteen. In some countries you can get married younger, with your parents' consent. Like going on a school excursion, all you need is a permission note:

Dear _____

I/We _____ *give our son* _____

permission to get married to _____

next Saturday at 3 o'clock. I/We understand that while all care is given, no responsibility is taken.

He will make his own way home from the registry and will not be requiring a packed lunch. Please find enclosed money to cover all costs.

Medication?: _____

Allergies?: _____

Signed: _____ *Dated:* _____

I reckon, though, that you'd have to be some kind of extra-special guy to get married at sixteen. When I was 16, I was a blithering idiot in the presence of anything even vaguely female. Also, statistically, the odds are not in your favour. Just look at what happened to Romeo and Juliet.

All this is fine in theory, but what about real life?

The word 'marriage' means lots of things to different people and carries with it a variety of connotations. Bridal magazines and wedding web-sites contain a panoply of romantic photographs and images: the elegantly clad bride in white, gliding down the aisle; candles, roses, vintage cars with silver ribbons; diamond rings, stained-glass windows, silver cutlery gleaming on crisp white tablecloths; the newlyweds driving away from a waving crowd; the bride staring at flowers in front of a frosted window; the handsome square-jawed groom laughing with his handsome square-jawed mates; the bridal party frolicking on a beach at sunset; lots of frilly borders that I don't know the name of; and, for some reason, everything gold-embossed in olde English fonts.

Marriage looks pretty good like that, doesn't it? It's all wonderful and appealing and romantic, isn't it? You can see yourself in that picture, can't you?

But I have some important news for you.

All that romantic stuff is NOT what marriage is about. All that romantic stuff is just window-dressing. Froth and bubble. Cream on the cake.

Sure, your wedding is a special occasion and it's fitting to indulge in the formality and finery of the day. It's appropriate to go to a lot of bother and spend a bit of money to make your wedding day special and memorable.

But a 'wedding' and a 'marriage' are not synonymous.

A *wedding* is an event that lasts a couple of hours — just long enough to say vows, eat some food and drink champagne. A wedding is a *ritual*.

A *marriage* is a relationship that is supposed to last 'till death do you part'. A marriage is a *lifestyle*.

Unfortunately, some people who contemplate marriage get sidetracked by the glitz of the wedding day itself, rather than focusing on the reality of the years ahead. They think more about champagne toasts and three-tiered cakes than about the serious implications of resolving conflict, managing money or bringing up children.

This was illustrated beautifully in an excessively stupid radio stunt a few years ago, where two listeners 'won' each other as husband and wife. The station paid for all the trimmings for an over-the-top wedding service and reception. Callers phoned in every day and everyone thought it was all very romantic. TV shows started covering it.

The day came, and amongst much fanfare the two strangers were wed.

Unfortunately, no-one thought ahead about what would happen when the public circus died down and the newlyweds were left with just each other. When their divorce was announced on air a few months later, some callers were genuinely shocked. One caller even said, 'If a marriage can't stay together after a fairytale wedding day like that, what hope have the rest of us got?' (Scary, isn't it?)

Getting married is a big step. Possibly one of the biggest steps you will ever take... unless you step into an elevator that's not there and you plummet forty storeys. *That's* a big step.

But I digress.

Marriage is bigger than changing jobs or moving house or winning a grand final against unbelievable odds.

Marriage is a way of life with enormous long-term consequences.

When you marry a woman, you are promising to be her companion for life; to love her and honour her and be sexually faithful to her; to make sacrifices and surrender some of your individual rights, privileges and freedoms. You are making a commitment to serve her, even when you don't feel like it — not just now when she's young and sexy and life is good, but in all the years to come, when you're losing your hair and she's putting on weight and work is stressful and the mortgage is crippling and life seems to have more downs than ups.

As the traditional service says, it is not a step to be taken lightly. Rather, it is one to be considered carefully, solemnly and seriously.

So, before you get too caught up in the romantic peripherals, think very carefully about making this big step.

Think carefully about the vows, statements and promises you want to say to the woman you love, probably in front of a frighteningly large assembly of friends and relatives. And ask yourself whether it's really what you want.

If you've still got it in your head that marriage is all kisses and roses, get your hands on a copy of Christopher Reeve's autobiography *Still Me*, published by Random House.

This is Reeve's sobering but inspiring story of how he and his family coped with his severe spinal injury after an accident in 1995. He and his wife were a highly successful couple and Reeve, as the actor who in four of his 18 films played Superman, had one of the most well known faces on the planet. Then, during an equestrian event, he was thrown from his horse, instantly severing his spinal cord and leaving him with no movement below the neck. He couldn't even breathe without the help of a machine.

Reeve tells of how, after surgery, he realised his life would never be the same again. He would always be a tremendous burden. When his wife Dana came in, she looked at him and he mouthed the words, 'Maybe we should let me go.'

For the couple, life as they knew it was over. There would be no more walks on the beach or impromptu nights out, no more sports or holding hands or candlelit dinners or flash celebrity parties. His career and their sex life, and pretty well everything else they had known and taken for granted, were all things of the past. Ahead of them lay tremendous financial burdens and a life in which simple things like toileting, eating, bathing and getting out of bed would take herculean effort.

But Dana squared herself up and said, 'I am only going to say this once: I will support whatever you want to do, because this is your life and your decision. But I want you to know that I'll be with you for the long haul, no matter what. You're still you. And I love you.'

Here is a model of a loving couple with a strong and committed relationship. They have overcome unbelievable adversity and Dana has put into practice the traditional wedding vows, 'for better or for worse'.

Still interested?

Read on, Macduff.

Marriage: Why would you?

> *By all means marry; if you get a good wife, you'll become happy. If you get a bad one, you'll become a philosopher.*
>
> SOCRATES

You're still here?
Good.
So now we know what marriage is, let's ask the next simple but obvious question.
Why?
Why would you do it?
In today's modern world of individuality, financial independence and sexual freedom, why would you opt for a monogamous relationship legally sanctified in an expensive public ceremony?
Evolutionary psychologists and sociology journals will tell you that you want to get married because marriage provides kudos and status; because it indicates you have been 'chosen'; because it enhances your self-esteem; because it is an anthropological extension of your primal 'mate-guarding' urges; because you have an innate need for permanence and security; because of normative conditioning and social pressure; because

Contemplation

... primal mate-guarding urges

of moral socialisation; because your partner has a high genetic potential for reproduction; because a committed relationship with a person of similar ideals provides you with emotional rewards; because (if you believe Freud) you've got the hots for your mum; because being in the presence of your partner releases opiates and amphetamines into your bloodstream. In short, because marriage makes you feel good.

Personally, these things weren't in my head when I was whacking a gold band on Meredith's finger and yelling out, 'I DO!' My reasons were not related to the cognitive-affective state characterised by obsessive and intrusive fantasising in relation to reciprocity of amorant feelings by the amorant object. No indeed. My reasons were less cerebral: I wanted to hang out with Meredith every day for the rest of my life. She made me laugh and was a good companion. We got on well and had interesting conversations. We liked the same things and shared a similar worldview. I admired her. I liked being with her even when we sat in silence. I wanted to impress her by catching footballs that had been kicked really high up in the air (the modern equivalent of coming home with a slain wildebeest and saying, 'Hey honey, look what I did!').

And to top it all off, she had this red swimming costume with a vertigo-inducing cleavage and a tie-thing at the back, and whenever she emerged dripping out of the surf, she did this hair-flicking routine which would bring a male rhino to...

Please excuse my aposiopesis.

No, there was no intellectual analysis of the motives behind my desire to get married. I did not have to talk myself into it or weigh up a list of the advantages and disadvantages. I didn't care if my cerebral cortex had been programmed in the primordial sludge by my ancestor, Thag Downey-Mammothconqueror III. I didn't care a Spanish fig for the high divorce rates. And I wasn't interested in simply 'moving in' together, either. I wanted the deluxe package, the whole caboose, the top tabouli, the burger with the lot.

It was the next logical step in our relationship...one which my brain and heart and Mr Percival all said was a damn good move. We were in love and we wanted to get married and that was that.

Besides, if she ever got with another guy, I'd rip his throat out with a fork and would end up in gaol as some cellmate's girlfriend.

Not an appealing thought.

Unfortunately, however, some people get married for the wrong reasons. They make a poor choice or have unsound motivations. Sure, they might survive the first few months or maybe even years on the momentum of the wedding extravaganza alone, but eventually they'll end up in the divorce courts.

Here is my list of 'really bad reasons to get married':

- *Sex.*

Your wife's personality and her companionship are the meat-and-three-veg of your marriage. Sex, on the other hand, is the cream on the cake at the end of the meal. It's real good, but you couldn't survive on it alone.

Sex is a great and vital part of a marriage, but your wife's not going to be 25 (or whatever) forever, and one day her hair will turn grey and gravity will attack her body and she'll no longer find the idea of 'doing it on the kitchen floor' an appealing prospect.

If you are getting married solely because:
a) your wife looks like a model, and
b) she is a predatory sexual banshee,
then your days are numbered.

- *As a prize in a radio competition.*

- *To try to get over an 'ex'.*

It is incomprehensible to me that anyone could be so stupid as to think that it's a good idea to throw yourself into marriage to help you recover from a previously failed relationship. Eventually your 'ex' will be long gone and you'll be left married to someone else. Very, very bad move.

- *Romance.*

Some people love 'being in love' ... the clammy hands and moonlit walks and flowers and kisses and poetry and glamour shots in bridal magazines. They are literally hooked on the rush of endorphins that comes from 'being in love'.

This is fine. All couples go through this, but the goo-goo eyes won't last forever. Sure, you'll still be 'in love' and there'll be plenty of romantic and erotic times, but you can't live in fairyland forever. Candlelit dinners in nice clothes at exclusive restaurants sipping shiraz will be balanced by sitting on the couch in tracksuits watching television and sipping hot chocolate. Walks in the park holding hands, kicking leaves and talking about how your love is as infinite as inky space will be balanced by doing the washing up and having mundane chats about replacing the filter system in your clothes dryer.

- *Political or financial gain.*

Some people do not marry for love or companionship but because it advances them in some way, perhaps because it gets them out of their social class or into a higher bracket of wealth, contact or power.

King Henry V, for example, invaded France, kicked butt at Agincourt, virtually wiped out the French nobility and demanded Princess Catherine as a marital 'payment'.

This is *not* the basis of a good marriage.

And while we may forgive the women in Jane Austen novels who got married as a necessity of nineteenth-century economic survival, it is hard to apply the same grace to today's massively bosomed blonde bimbettes who marry 90-year-old billionaires and claim that their love is genuine.

Eventually, the novelty of flashy cars, Dom Perignon and overseas skiing weekends will wear thin, and they'll realize that money can't buy happiness and that 'stuff' isn't so much fun when the price is getting into bed every night with a bloke older than their grandfather.

(Then again, you never hear the 90-year-olds complaining, so who am I to get all self-righteous?)

- *All your friends are getting married.*

In a close community or small group of friends, it's relatively easy to talk yourself into liking someone — maybe even into marrying them — because everyone else is doing it. There's a sense in which they're all moving on, which in turn promotes a fear that you will in some way be left behind.

This never works out in the long run.

- *You're hopeless at ironing and cooking and your mum and dad are sick of you.*

No, no, no, no, no.

Hopefully, you're not an idiot and your motives in wanting to have a long-term relationship with one woman are more noble and justifiable than any of the above.

But marriage just sounds like a lot of fuss. Why not just live together?

Good question.

It's true that in this day and age, more people live together without first going through the traditional engagement/wedding ceremony than at any other point in history. In fact, about 50% of all couples walking down the aisle today have already been living together.

So why do they bother, then? If you're already living as a married couple, why go back to the proverbial Square One and dress up and have a big public hoo-ha celebrating something you did long ago?

Lots of reasons.

For many, the 'living together' thing is a trial run. Couples are more cynical and cautious about marriage, what with the divorce rate and all. Many were brought up in single-parent homes and are therefore first-hand witnesses to a failed marriage. These people are less likely to dive headfirst into the deep end from the 5-metre board without first testing the water temperature with their big toe.

And so, like a 30-day money-back guarantee on a digital watch, they move in together, just to check it out, to see if it works. If it doesn't, it's relatively easy just to walk out.

While some couples view this as a permanent lifestyle arrangement, I suspect most are wanting to test and confirm their suspicion that 'it' will work with this particular person and that they are, in fact, the right one for the marital job.

I have done no particular research into this, but according to my lived-together-before-getting-married friends with whom I discussed this issue (over several bottles of red wine...), there *is* a difference between being married and simply living with someone.

Their reasons for getting married were:

1. They were technically already married (de facto) in the eyes of the law, so from there it was not such a big step to formalise things on paper. They had already proven their relationship mettle, so marriage was no longer something to be scared of.

2. Shifting their focus from the 'now' to the 'future', these couples wanted more than a casual arrangement. Their levels of romantic, social and economic attachment had developed to such a degree that they wanted a more permanent situation with a greater level of security. While acknowledging that a marriage

certificate itself has no magical properties, they had mentally moved to the point of viewing a public marriage ceremony as a reflection of their already permanent relationship.

3. They wanted to make more of a serious and formal public declaration about their relationship, rather than an unceremonious, 'I've moved in with Chris, here's my new phone number…'

4. After a while, the reproductive/nesting gene kicked in and the spectre of children raised its whining head. (Leaving political correctness aside, and assuming that no brave new world suddenly emerges, the fact is that the married couple remains the dominant form of family arrangement for raising children.)

5. It was unfair that they were living like a married couple (heated discussions over bill payments, household chores, in-law disputes, fights over whose razor is whose) without reaping any of the celebratory benefits (bucks'/hens' nights, engagement party, nice wedding service with photos and dressing up, lots of presents, an elegant reception and honeymoon in a beachfront bungalow).

Oh, there was also one guy whose partner's father said that if he didn't marry his daughter within 12 months of moving in together, he'd have some blokes do him over with a range of bats from a variety of sports.

2
Engagement
(the fun bit)

'I remember the night I asked Kerry to marry me. I was sick with worry. What if I got the signals wrong and she said "no", or "Give me a few days"? We drove up to a lookout and she must have known it was on, because I was babbling like an idiot. I'm not a nervous person, but the rest of my life was hanging on the next few minutes. She said yes before I'd even finished my awkward little speech. It was one of the best moments of my life.'

ANDY, 25

Popping the question

He asked me to marry him between the powdered soup and the croutons. I let him stew for a week, then I said yes.

JULIE

David took Joanne to an elegant harbour restaurant for brunch. They sat on the balcony over the water where, like in a dream, the sun danced lazily over Joanne's face and silky hair.

A stretch limo drove them to the airport where they took their first-class seats on an interstate flight for a matinée performance of the musical *Rent*. Best seats in the house. When the applause of the final curtain call had faded, they walked to an exclusive restaurant just in time for their dinner reservation. There they feasted on sumptuous and rare dishes. David ordered a bottle of Grange. Their conversation flowed like the tide to the rhythm of the string quartet.

Afterwards, in the hire car David had arranged to have left outside the restaurant, they drove to a lookout he had often visited as a child. There, under the inky blanket of stars, he drew Joanne close to him and pressed his lips to hers. He gently pulled back and stared into the eternal pools of her eyes. With his heart audibly pounding in his ears, he whispered his now immortal words, 'Jo, will you marry me?'

Joanne stared back, took a breath and whispered *her* now immortal word, 'No.'

True story.

All up, a really lousy end to an otherwise very nice day. Aside from getting the negatory marital flick-pass, it also put a rapid end to their relationship...to say nothing of the substantial ding in Dave's bank account.

If you're going to pop the question, then I hope you've got at least some vague semblance of a notion of a vibe that the answer will be 'yes'. Maybe hints have been dropped or you've discussed it in a roundabout way already?

Eventually, if you want to take the lead in the whole deal, you're going to have to ask her the big question. While I don't think that you need to go so far as a colleague of mine — who had arranged for one passenger at each of 12 consecutive bus stops to step aboard the bus and deliver his girlfriend a single red rose, only to have him hop on the bus at the 13th stop and propose, in front of 75 sardined passengers — you should at least have thought about the words you are going to use and make them at least half-decent and memorable, like, '[Insert name here], I love you and I want to spend the rest of my life with you. You complete me; you're a top chick. Will you marry me?'

If she *ums* and *ahs*, add this little beauty: 'I need to know tonight, because if it's "no" I've got a couple of other girls lined up.' *Never fails.*

And whatever you do, don't subscribe to the pathetic movie stereotype of the getting-down-on-one-knee-in-a-crowded-restaurant routine. It looks good on the big screen, but in real life it's not so nice for all the other diners who are trying to stomach their food while you carry on like a couple of dogs on heat. That's to say nothing of the embarrassment you'll experience if, instead of her responding, 'I thought you'd never ask...Oh, I love you so much...I don't know what to say...I mean yes, the answer's yes. I want to share the rest of my life with you,' and everybody claps and cheers and the waiter brings champagne and declares that your meal tonight is 'on the house, courtesy of Luigi', she gets coy and teary and says something along the lines of, 'Well look, I'll have to...um...think about it ...Why did you have to do it here? Why did you ...I never thought that...I need time to think. I'm so embarrassed...' and then someone in the kitchen drops a stack of plates.

Let's be honest. This is a 'no'.

While I'm thinking of it, the whole 'buying the ring before you ask her' thing is to be avoided at all costs. You're bound to get the size and style wrong. But that, of course, leads to a whole nightmarish adventure of its own — shopping for an engagement ring. This is where you get to put your credit card where your mouth is and show the depth of your love. Hopefully, your bride will have a sense of self-respect and good taste and she will not want a rock the size of a meteorite pulling her arm out of its socket.

But be prepared to pay. According to De Beers, the average engagement ring should cost around two months salary. (Of course, being a diamond merchant, they would say that!) At the opposite extreme, I met a woman once who had a colourful plastic engagement ring that they bought for ten bucks in an op-shop. It looked crappy to me, but she treasured it like it was titanium.

Many people are creative in their wedding proposals.

One mate of mine filled their flat (they were living together) with roses. She came home from work, read the note telling her to look out the window, and there he was, holding a placard that said: 'Marriage? Say *yes*.'

I know another guy who dubbed the movie *Four Weddings and a Funeral* onto a videotape and, in the middle, inserted a little self-filmed footage. One Saturday night, eating pizza and watching the movie in her darkened lounge room, they were in the middle of one of the wedding ceremonies when he suddenly appeared on the screen, saying something like, 'Help! Help! I'm stuck in this film and the only way I can get out is if some highly intelligent and attractive woman marries me. Is there anybody out there? Hey you...yeah you. Will you marry me?'

... some kind of regal proposal

Stories of other wacky proposals abound.

I have heard of the guy who arranged a skywriter proposal to his girlfriend (and ten thousand others) while they were at the beach; the guy who proposed to his girlfriend live on FM radio; the guy who sent a singing telegram to his girlfriend's work; the guy who designed a 'marry me' website for his girlfriend; the guy who made a 'Will you marry me?' sign out of 180 light bulbs and left it in her driveway one night; and of course, the guy who tattooed 'Marry me!' on his massive... oh, never mind.

A proposal is only limited by your finances, imagination, personality, sense of good taste and common decency.

Then again, it may not be *you* popping the question.

Yes, it's unbelievable but true, but all your grand plans and thoughts about making some sort of regal proposal might come to a crashing halt when one day, in the middle of a tennis match, your girlfriend calls out, 'Do you want to get married?'

Alternatively, there might be no grand question popping at all but rather a *discussion* on the topic. I know a couple who had lived together for five years and one night they both for some reason woke up and started talking about it and decided to get married three months later. Then they went back to sleep.

My own wedding proposal was less than romantic.

Meredith and I were playing chess. She was 20, I was twenty-three. I said something like, 'I hope we'll still be playing chess 20 years from now.'

'Yeah, that'd be nice,' she said.

'Do you think we will?'

'Yeah.'

'You mean...do you reckon...'

'Yeah.'

King's pawn two.

'Like, what are you talking about?'

'You know...you and...um...me. Um, 20 years...'

'What?'

'Huh?'

'What...Are you talking about a thing that starts with "M"?'

'Yeah.'

Queen's bishop five.

'You mean mud wrestling?'

'No.'

'Morris dancing?'

'This is getting boring...'

'Oh! Like a *mar ... riag ... ey* kind of thing?'

'Yeah.'

'Do you reckon we ever will?'

'Yeah.'

'Yeah?'

'Yeah.'

Queen to knight's pawn three.

'When?'

'What?'

'When?'

'I dunno...Are we talking sooner...or...later?'

'Um, sooner?'

'Like...um...next year sooner, or five years sooner?'

'I dunno. What d'you think?'
'I dunno...next year?'
'Yeah. When next year?'
'I dunno...December?'
'December...yeah.'
King to Queen's bishop one.
'So that's it, then?'
'Yep.'
'Are we...um...engaged then?'
'I guess so.'
Bishop to cardinal's maid's brother's thirteen.
'So...we're getting married? That's it, then.'
'Yeah, we're getting married. Checkmate.'
'That's it, then.'
'Yeah.'
Pretty riveting stuff. And to think, on the basis of this conversation over a simple game of chess, came the best years of my life.

Going public

We announced our engagement and within five days we had booked up 13 weeks of dinner parties.

ROGER

Once you and the love of your life have decided to get married, there are a number of people you will want to tell. Obviously, a decision to get married is not something you casually let slip out in a 'Could you please pass the caesar salad, and oh, by the way, did I happen to mention...' moment.

No indeed.

A matter of such import requires more consideration.

I had a long-standing fear of speaking to my girlfriend's parents about marriage ever since I saw a movie where an anxious beau confronted his girlfriend's cantankerous father and awkwardly mumbled something like, 'Mr Pennington, I wonder if I might have a moment of your time, sir. You see, it's like this. Jordanalli and me... well, we been courting for some time now ...and I love her, Mr Pennington, honest I do. And now that I've got a good job down at the mill, I'd like to ask for ... gee, Mr Pennington, this is harder than I thought ... But I'd be right pleased if I could have your daughter's hand in marriage...'

I dreaded the day when I would eventually have to front up to Meredith's father. This was not helped by the cruel twist of fate that caused him to look like a cross between a bouncer and a lumberjack. I lived in constant fear that he would find us smooching on their back doorstep, snap me into three pieces and shoot each of them individually into the basketball hoop on their driveway.

But I had a brief reprieve because we didn't tell anyone our news for two weeks. We knew our friends and family would go berserk, so we wanted some time to get used to the idea privately before having to cope with the public circus. We were able to discuss a number of issues and ideas about weddings and married life without everyone else intruding with their opinions.

We enjoyed each day, knowing that we would be married the next December, and like little children harbouring a naughty secret, relished the fact that no-one else knew. I can thoroughly recommend such a temporary cone of silence over your marital intentions.

But the cat has to be let out eventually.

Protocol dictates that parents are told first. An announcement of such gravity should be delivered face to face — which is fine if, like us, your parents live a few kilometres away. But if they live interstate or in the Nepalese highlands, a phone call will do. Writing a letter should be a last resort, although it is preferable to a fax or email, which is only acceptable if you live on an Antarctic icefloe.

Traditionally, the groom asks the bride's parents 'for her hand'. (While you're at it, I suggest you try to acquire a good portion of her upper torso as well.) And may you do a better job than James Somersby who, in 1908, visited his love's parents to ask for her hand, but after spilling ink on a priceless tapestry and sitting on the family Pekinese (causing instantaneous death-by-buttock to the poor dog) was, not surprisingly, unsuccessful.

In today's not-so-patriarchally-condescending world, most grooms don't actually 'ask' the bride's parents for *permission* to get married, in the true sense of the word...as in that if they said 'no', he'd just wander home with his tail between his legs. Most couples simply declare their intentions, especially if they're already living together. But if you're smart, you'll seek some sort of approval, blessing or endorsement from the family. Such support is very desirable in the years to come, especially if the bride's father is an ex-wrestler with a red face and veins that stick out of his forehead.

I clearly remember the night we broke our good news to our parents.

I experienced a strange mix of excitement and nervousness, which is understandable given that I had no prior experience in trying to snatch a daughter away from her parents.

We told Meredith's parents first. After a lengthy dinner-table discussion about the various merits of natural gas over electricity, I skilfully segued into a spiel about our friendship and commitment and how our relationship was ready to burst forth like a butterfly from its cocoon, and eventually I made it to the bit where I told them, if it was all right with them, that I wanted to marry their daughter.

Fortunately, our respective parents were pleased and supportive. Meredith's dad hit me so hard on the back that I needed physio the next morning. Her mum was also very pleased, but reminded me that her daughter still had a year of uni to go, and that if I made her leave tertiary study to have babies and cook dinners, she'd be after me with a breadknife.

My parents got a blunter version. Right in the middle of the seven o'clock news, I blurted out, 'We're getting married.'

My mum clapped her hands together and headed for the fridge to rummage for champagne. My dad yelled out, 'What'd he say?' and told me to get out of the line of sight between him and the television.

If you are travelling overseas or interstate to meet your fiancée's parents for the first time, this is obviously going to be a very significant occasion.

One that should be handled well.

First impressions count, and your introduction is very important. Your future in-laws will want to know that you are a loving, stable man with a solid income and high levels of personal hygiene and grooming. They will want to be reassured that you will be a devoted and caring husband with plans to soon provide them with a houseful of grandchildren.

Whatever you do at this first meeting, don't slap their daughter on the butt and refer to her as 'babe' or 'the little lady'; don't wink at the mother every time she speaks to you; don't ask if you can borrow $100 'to see you through'; don't sigh a lot and talk about your ex-girlfriends; and don't give them a presentation to try to convince them to join your latest networking-direct-marketing venture.

But now the game's afoot and you have to work quickly. Wedding news spreads faster than the bubonic plague. If you want to tell people personally, rather than have them hear on the grapevine, you don't have a moment to spare. It only takes one multiple email and everyone you have ever met in your entire life will know that you are getting married before you've even lifted the receiver.

At best, you can hope to tell a handful of your closest friends and relatives in person and maybe a few more by phone. You've got one or two days, tops.

If you've got heaps of friends, family and business associates, whip up a nice 'Announcing...!' flier with a photo of both of you and email or post it around.

I really enjoyed breaking the news. We had a ball declaring to all and sundry that we were going to take the big step...drinking champagne, watching the look on their faces, drinking champagne, receiving their hearty congratulations, drinking champagne, feeling slightly off-colour, drinking champagne, trembling at their leery threats in relation to the bucks' night, drinking champagne, discussing our wedding plans, drinking champagne, watching the room spin, drinking champagne, falling to my knees, drinking champagne, vomiting, vowing never to drink champagne again.

I also enjoyed telling all my ex-girlfriends. Sure, my mouth was saying, 'Meredith and I are getting married,' but my brain was saying, 'Hey baby, look what you missed out on.'

And so we spent several days enjoying celebratory drinks, impromptu dinners, late-night port toastings and generally being the centre of attention.

Enjoy this time.

Enjoy telling your family and friends.

Enjoy settling in to the idea of marriage.

Because from here on in, the whole thing gets way out of control. You have just entered another dimension: a dimension of dinner parties, a dimension of long planning sessions. You have just entered...the engagement zone.

And your life will never be the same again.

So, you're engaged

If marriage is like buying a car, then the engagement is like an 18-month spin around the block to see how it handles.

PETER DOWNEY

The Saturday after we 'went public', Meredith and I went to a twenty-first birthday bash. I can't remember whose it was, but I remember that it was in someone's backyard and there was loud music, a smoky barbecue and a comprehensive selection of cheeses.

As we queued for the marinated chicken wings and beetroot salad on paper plates, we started talking to a couple we'd never met before. I said, 'By the way, I'm Peter and this is my…'

Unexpectedly, I paused.

Usually I would just have said, '… and this is my girlfriend Meredith.'

But the rules had changed.

She wasn't *just my girlfriend* any more; she was more than that. We planned to spend the rest of out lives together, damn it. The term 'girlfriend' didn't convey the newfound weight of our relationship and the magnitude of our familial destiny.

So for the first time in my life, my mouth had to get around the word 'fiancée'.

Fiancée.

Go on, say it.

Fee-ON-say.

Takes a bit of getting used to, doesn't it? Like your mouth is full of pebbles.

To be honest, I felt a bit self-conscious calling Meredith my 'fiancée', as if everybody standing within earshot would leer at us and yell, 'Oooohhh...luuuu-vers. Getting maaaar-reeeeed.'

Seems silly now. If I had my time again, it'd be no big deal. I'd probably just say, '...and this is Meredith.'

But something still didn't sit right.

The problem was, we were planning to get married but were not married. We loved each other and wanted to spend the rest of our lives together, but we weren't there yet.

We were in a twilight zone, a grey area, a no-man's-land between a time of our lives that hadn't quite gone and a time of our lives that hadn't quite started.

When you are in this zone of life, you are 'engaged' — as in 'engaged to be married'.

And in the very early days of this 'engagement', things change. The tectonic plate of your relationship has to move and it takes a while for it to really sink in that, after all this time, you're going to be married.

But it's not just you.

People start treating you differently. Your married friends and distant married cousins start asking you over for dinner. It's like you've joined their special club or something.

Aside from freeloading nice food and wine off your friends, this engagement period does actually have a purpose.

Think about it.

How come, once you decide to get married, you don't simply whack the ring on the finger right there and then? I mean, what's the point of mucking about? It seems like a waste of time, doesn't it? Like saying you're going to buy a car...but not until 5 pm in another eight months' and six days' time.

There are four reasons why marriage is not instantaneous:
1. Legally, you can't get married on the spot.

You have to 'give notice' to the person marrying you (priest, celebrant, rabbi, registrar, etc) and allow a certain period to pass before the day. The time varies from community to community, but for some bizarre reason it's generally a month and a day.

That is, unless you live in Vegas, where an Elvis impersonator will fix you up with a nifty five-minute wedding in a drive-through chapel. *Now that's class!*

... unless you live in Vegas

2. You need a cool-down period.

Like buying a multi-vascular super-work-out 50-machines-in-one home gymnasium ('Look like *this* in just two minutes a day, with absolutely *no* effort! Incredible!') from a late-night infomercial, sometimes you regret decisions made in the heat of the moment. Sure, at 3 am when you couldn't sleep and you dialled the number on your screen ('within the next three minutes so you can get this bonus cassette to expand your memory by 6000% and give you the personal power to take control of your own life and walk across hot coals and breathe fire and discover unlimited wealth and increase your cup size to DD and our hot girls are waiting to talk to you now'), it all seemed to make perfect sense. But the next morning you realise you're an idiot.

See, there's a difference between vaguely fantasising about getting married in an abstract sense and actually doing it. Sure, getting married might have seemed wonderfully romantic when you and your lady were sitting in front of a log fire in a hut in the snow drinking red wine... but when you get back to the cold hard reality of life in a red-brick mortgage for the next 50 years, you might have second thoughts.

So this 'engagement' gives the two of you a bit of time to stare at your navels and seriously consider what you're doing. It gives you the opportunity to test the water and see if you're going to float or drown. It allows you the luxury of making sure that this important decisions has not been made in the heat of the moment.

I know three couples who called their weddings off during their engagements. Once they upped the ante in their relationship, they came to realise that it wasn't what they wanted. This saddened me, not because their weddings didn't go ahead, but because not one of them gave back the cheese platters I gave them as engagement presents.

3. If you are not already living together, starting a new life can't be whipped up as quickly as, say, changing your shoes.

There are one squintillion tasks to be done, from the massively monumental to the irritatingly insignificant: from searching Saturday classifieds looking for a new place to live, to filling out 'change of address' forms at your bank; from attempting to resolve your different attitudes towards family roles and household chores, to discussing the logistical advantages of having a four-slice toaster with crumpet facility over a two-slice toaster with auto-browner.

4. The *real* reason behind the engagement (you read it here first, folks!) is so you can plan a whiz-bang wedding service, reception and honeymoon.

Those three-tier fruitcakes with marzipan icing sure take some organising!

Learning the ropes

Happiness in marriage is entirely a matter of chance ... it is better to know as little as possible of the defects of the person with whom you are to pass your life.

CHARLOTTE LUCAS IN JANE AUSTEN'S
PRIDE AND PREJUDICE.

Imagine that you are going on an overseas trip.

A big one. A once-in-a-lifetime holiday.

You've got six months off work and you plan to travel to the farthest reaches, climb every mountain, cross every stream, chase the sun, span the largest metaphors — you get the picture.

This trip is going to be such a big deal, in fact, that you decide to hold the going-away party to end all going-away parties.

You spend months planning the party. The preparations are extravagant. The guest list is endless. There's a colour scheme, nice invitations, fine foods and wines, speeches, and of course a photographer to record the event for posterity.

The big day arrives and it's a tremendous (albeit expensive) success.

The next day, you go to the airport. And it's only then that you realise you spent so much time planning your going-away party that you forgot to think about the holiday. You forgot to pack. But that doesn't matter, because you don't have a plane ticket anyway. Nor do you have a passport, traveller's cheques, hotel reservations, magazines for in-flight reading or an inflatable pillow. In fact, you have no idea where you were going to go anyway.

Sure, you should have planned your trip a little better, but at the time, the grade of paper you used on your party invitations seemed really important.

Okay, it's a stupid analogy, but I'm sure you get the point. Preparing for your wedding day takes up a lot of time, thought and energy.

For months, the main topics of conversation will be whether you'll have the prawn or chicken entrée and whether Sid and Julie would be better sitting next to your Uncle Jack (who thinks that all people under 30 are unemployed and have pierced navels) or next to Moira and Carlo (who love to tell strangers about their plans to renovate their house).

The great irony is that in all this preparation for the wedding ceremony, not many couples spare more than a moment's thought about the marriage itself... which is a bit cart-before-the-horse, if you think about it.

If you value something and want to be good at it, you work hard to prepare for it. You take instruction from your driving instructor. You listen carefully to the guy attaching the bungee rope to your feet. You ask questions of the traveller who has gone before you. You follow your accountant's advice.

But what do you do if you want to be a successful *husband*? Given that your marriage is probably one of the most significant events in your life, what *training* do you do for it?

Probably none.

You will not have graduated from 'Marriage 101' at school. There are no uni qualifications in matrimony. My guess is you haven't read a single book on relationships. And sadly for a significant number of us, the home has failed to provide an appropriate husband role model.

And so, many couples are ill-prepared for marriage.

Once upon a time, the definition of pre-marital advice was your drunk Uncle Kevin taking you aside and saying, 'Mate, the secret to a happy wife is to let her spend as much as she wants on shoes. Shoes and the occasional slap'n'tickle and she'll be in the palm of your hand...'

Today, fortunately, things are a little different.

Now there are many community, government and religious organisations which offer courses to help you prepare more carefully for your marriage.

Don't be put off by the word 'course'. They're not new-age encounter groups where you light candles and get in touch with your inner child. Nor are they lectures with some old grunter standing at a lectern prattling on about 'the ten steps to a successful marriage'.

Rather, marriage courses are designed to help you contemplate your relationship in a structured format. They focus on your attitudes, emotions and expectations of marriage and each other, and raise many issues worth discussing.

Some courses last a few sessions, others are weekend retreats. Some offer group discussions or role-plays, while others demand little more than the filling out of a long questionnaire and having a chat with a facilitator. Topics covered usually include sex, work, home life, chores, family, children, friends, finances, conflict resolution, communication, religion and how to decide on a restaurant without having a major fight. These are important issues that you may not have even considered.

It was at our marriage course, for example, that I first discovered Meredith's desire to have seven children, and she discovered my inability to function unless my sock drawer is ordered by colour.

In some circumstances, courses or questionnaires have led to couples postponing their wedding or calling it off altogether. One of the individuals — or both of them — realises that there is a point of incompatibility in their relationship, like when he 'fesses up that a wife's job is to leave the workforce, get pregnant and serve him beer, or when she expresses her anticipation at getting access to his credit card because her lifelong goal is to have more shoes than Imelda Marcos.

Splitting up is never nice, but it's much better to do it *before* than *after* the whole rigmarole of the wedding.

A marriage course is the best way to safeguard against nasty post-nuptial surprises, and you won't freak out when your wife says: 'Are you kidding? Children?' or 'I just can't save any money — as soon as it's in the account, I have to spend it' or 'But I always assumed Grandma would come to live with us!' or 'Yes, I'm angry with you, but I can't bring myself to talk about it... at least, not for six months, anyway...' or 'Listen, look at it from Hitler's point of view.'

3
Preparations

(the spin-out)

'We had a great wedding. It was a fantastic day and everyone enjoyed themselves.

But not too many people knew about the eight months of sheer, unadulterated hell that had gone into organising it. I never realised people felt so strongly about weddings. Lisa and I disagreed on quite a few things — nothing major — but enough to cause some tears. That was before our parents even came into the equation. They wanted this, they wanted that. They wanted different things from each other. It was like trying to manage the United Nations, but nobody was sure who the President was.'

AKIRA, 30

Get involved

Men differ from women. You never see young men sitting around talking about their dream wedding.

CHARLES COSART

You are at Point A.

Point A is where you and your fiancée have agreed to get married.

As in, to each other.

As in, on a certain day in the future...known as Point B.

Between Point A and Point B there is a lot of work to be done. Make no mistake about this. A medium-scale wedding is only slightly less complex to organise than, say, a military invasion of a neighbouring country.

A wedding doesn't just happen. You can't simply turn up and wing it on the day (well you could, I guess, but let's be honest, it'd be a crap wedding).

For your wedding day to run smoothly, there are decisions to be made — from the big, earth-shatteringly important ones, right down to the stupid, piddly, who-gives-a-rat's-arse kind of decisions. There are discussions to be discussed with all and sundry persons of relevance. There are bookings to be booked and payments to be paid. There are people to be seen and negotiations to be negotiated, and annoying family politics to be kept in a fine balance. There are fights and disagreements to be had, and sulking and raised voices to be apologised for. And then there is an enormous wedding-day timetable to be constructed between 6 am (go for an early surf with the lads) and 11.45 pm (put on cowboy outfit and jump out of the bathroom).

Start the process *earlier* rather than *later* to give you more flexibility and so there'll be fewer last-minute frantic decisions to be made.

Early organisation gives you more time to research, discuss and plan the wedding you want, as well as increasing your access to services that require pre-booking and deposits, like the reception venue, the church/celebrant, photographer, cars, hotel, stripper, suit hire, honeymoon, flights and full-body wax.

There is a lot to be done.

But who is supposed to do what?

The great marital god Tradition has some very strong opinions on the matter. Wedding books and marriage websites invariably have their own very specific and detailed lists and protocols about which people are responsible for what.

To be honest, I don't think there's any place for such lists in the rapidly changing world of marriage. These lists represent dinosaur philosophies of antiquated marriage roles that hark from previous generations.

For example, most lists make no mention at all of the groom's parents — except for one that said, 'They are the honoured guests who sit in the front row. If convenient, they may like to help in *some* of the arrangements.'

That hardly seems fair.

One website said that 'the bride's mother is the key person in all wedding arrangements'.

Why should the mother of the bride have her fingers in every pie? What makes her so special?

The same regimented traditions apply to who pays for which parts of the wedding. Essentially, it's the bride's parents and the groom who have to cough up the dough. The groom's parents and the bride herself seem to get off scot free, which might have made good sense 200 years ago when the bloke was the wage-earner and the woman was the child-rearer, but in this day and age that doesn't seem to make much sense. If we live in an era of equal rights where you're not even supposed to let a woman through a door first because that implies she's inferior, how come she doesn't have to pay for anything at her own wedding?

As I said, traditional wedding protocol is contradictory, inconsistent and out of date. It fails to take into account the tremendous variety of circumstances surrounding a contemporary wedding. For one thing, many couples are marrying later in life and they may have been 'out of home' and financially independent for a number of years. On top of that, many couples are already living together when they get married, and Mum and Dad aren't necessarily going to want to buy into the big marital investment after all these years, just because the kids finally decide to hitch up and have a big party.

I think it's time we broke the bonds of tradition. You and your fiancée (and/or your families) should organise your wedding your own way, according to your own circumstances and situation. Planning and payment should be shared out or negotiated, not just assigned to various members because of allegiance to some outmoded tradition printed in a book with roses and a diamond ring on the front cover.

And another thing...

Many of these wedding lists put you, the groom, way down the organisational pecking order. All you have to supposedly do is hire a suit, buy a ring, turn up, look good, get married, sign the register, be in the photos, cut the cake, waltz, make a speech and leave.

Of course, you may be quite happy taking a back seat in your wedding preparations. You may baulk at all the work that needs to be done on the line between Point A and Point B. Some guys abdicate their responsibility and develop a shoulder-shrugging 'do whatever you want and I'll see you on the day' attitude.

Let me encourage you *not* to do this.

Take a front seat.

Preparations

Speak up.
Be an active participant in your wedding.
There are four reasons for this:
1. It's your wedding. You have a right to have your say, damn it.
2. It's your bride's wedding too: you have a responsibility not to dump all the work onto her. It's just not fair, for one thing, and for another it will not endear you to her in terms of your attitude toward getting your hands dirty later in your married life.
3. Taking an active role will help you look forward to the wedding more. Spend time going over the preparations, and think of the relief you'll feel when those sleepless, sweaty-sheeted, how-can-we-afford-this/no-we're-not-inviting-HER/I-hate-marzipan nights are over.
4. If you don't speak up, somebody else will be making decisions for you... and that person might have shocking taste. Do you really want duelling tubas played as you walk down the aisle in a purple velour jumpsuit? Besides, they might have no concept of that magic and all-important word, 'budget'.

Sorry. I've been leading you astray. Reading back over these paragraphs, I can see that you might have perceived that I have implied that you are in some way in charge of your wedding day.
That all marital power lies with you.
That your wedding day is a dominion over which you are sovereign.
Wrong.
Do not pass go.
Do not collect $200.
But more of that on the next pages...

I thought this was <u>my</u> wedding

*I drew the line when my father-in-law phoned up to ask
if I was wearing braces or a belt.*

ANTONIO

You may be under the misapprehension that your wedding belongs to you. That is it's *about* you and *for* you.
 You may have a picture in your head that you are up in the cockpit at the controls of your marital Lear jet, pressing all the buttons and making all the decisions. You know... cruising at 30 000 feet, the cabin crew will be round in a minute to serve coffee and light refreshments, and if we lose pressure this plastic mask will fall down from the roof and donk you on the head.
 Wrong.
 If you look carefully at that picture, you will notice that there are several pairs of hands on your joystick trying to push it this way and that. And half the emergency lights in the cockpit are flashing red.
 You see, my dear friend, you are not the pilot.
 What you are, in actual fact, is the head flight attendant. You wear a smart suit, shake hands at the door, stand up the front where everyone can see you, say a few words and, on their way

out, thank them all for coming. Sure, you can pop up into the cockpit for a visit, but you ain't pressing the big buttons.

Nearly always, there are other people and other forces vying for control. Let's have a look at each of these in turn.

Bride

As you walk down the road of Wedding Preparation on your way to the Big Aisle, you will soon come face to face with one of the great universal truths: *The wedding day revolves around the bride.*

Make no mistake. Men and women have different perceptions and expectations about weddings and marriage. Women have an entire sub-culture of marital ideas...a sub-culture, I might add, of which you have no concept.

Don't believe me?

Next time you go to a wedding, watch what happens when the bride walks in. The guys will stare at her with looks that say, *What took you so long?* and *Can I sit down now?* and *What time does the reception start anyway?*

At the same wedding, however, the women will start crying, sighing and snapping off roll after roll of photographs.

Or what about when you go to a wedding by yourself and afterwards a woman asks you about it? 'What was the bride wearing?' she asks, and you, panicking because you have no idea, answer, 'White.' Then she grills you about the sleeves, the hat, the veil, the train, the attendants, the make-up, the material, the neckline, the flower girls, the hair, and you're just thinking, *What the hell are you talking about?*

When was the last time one of your mates asked you what the *groom* was wearing? Morning suit? Bow-tie? What kind of shoes? Straight cut or flares? Grey, black or casual? And what did he do with his hair? *Eh?*

And what about at the newsagent? Compare all the 'bride magazines' to the 'groom magazines'...

Yeah, exactly.

If you're still under the illusion that the big day is yours just as much as it is hers, consider the cost factor. The guy hires a suit for a few bucks. It takes one fitting to work out the size. He wears his own shoes. As an extravagance, he lashes out and gets a buttonhole rose.

The bride, on the other hand, has bought, or had made, an expensive dress. And I *do* mean expensive. Ten fittings. It will be worn once.

The make-up artist doesn't come cheap, either. Neither does the hair stylist. Neither does the florist.

Add up the columns and talk to me about equality!

Here's the final proof of the pudding: when was the last time you went to a wedding where the woman waited up the front and the guy did the big walk down the aisle?

Yeah, I thought so.

(Notice, by the way, that the music is always 'Here Comes the Bride'. No-one's ever played 'Here Comes the Groom'.)

In short, the whole day puts the bride in the middle and everybody else on the periphery. Including you. Your shared wedding is really 'her day'.

Mums and dads

A mate of mine announced that he was going to get married. Pretty soon, all the preparations started.

One night he was having one of those let's-get-together-around-the-dining-room-table talks with his bride and both sets of parents. Nice cheeses and wines — you know the deal.

They were going through a whole lot of nitty-gritty stuff, and soon the discussion turned to wedding cars.

'Classic Rolls. Three of them. All silver,' hummed the bride's mother, her eyes moist and dreamy.

'Ah, well,' responded my mate, not wanting a confrontation with his mother-in-law-to-be but sensing that one was inevitable, 'Actually, Gloria, we don't want to hire wedding cars. Some of our old uni mates have got convertibles and we…'

Gloria's expression turned feral.

'…and we thought it would be kinda' cool…to…um…'

He was interrupted by the sound of Gloria's grinding teeth. Her pupils shrunk to pinpoints and the sickening smell of death filled the room.

Preparations

'...ride around in...um...convertibles.'

My mate's soon-to-be mother-in-law dug her fingernails into the mahogany table, leaned forward, and in a voice that left no doubt that her will was immutable, handed down this declaration: 'This may be *your* marriage, but it's *my* wedding.'

True story.

Normally, you'll be pleased to learn, most weddings aren't ruined by pushy parents. The majority of parents are reasonable people who listen to the bride and groom's wishes and discuss things openly ... *before* declaring that 'if there isn't a five-tiered fruitcake with marzipan icing, then you'd just better elope'.

One can't be too harsh on the parents (especially if they're paying). Because not only is a wedding a ritual of joining with another person and starting a new family unit, it is also a ritual of official farewell to the 'old' family. Regardless of whether you're already out of home and living with someone, or moving out of your old bedroom, many parents see a wedding as their farewell gesture and final financial responsibility.

All those years: those nappies and play nights and family holidays and birthday parties and school lunches and picking you up from training and teenage angst and sitting by your sickbed and finding your stash of porno mags under your bed and meeting your love for the first time... You can understand that, over time, they have developed a few ideas about the occasion which signals your departure from the nest.

I certainly have with my daughters. If I'm spending big bucks on a wedding, I don't want some 25-year-old fiancé telling me what to do. When my daughters get married there will be bagpipes, the limbo and cocktail franks with tomato sauce.

Your job as the groom is to work out what battles to fight... and what battles to surrender.

So your mum wants pink flowers on the tables? *Big deal!*

So her dad wants to perform a Gaelic dirge banjo version of 'Here comes the Bride'? *Not a problem!*

Save your combat energy for the issues over which you want to dig your heels in.

So her mum wants to come along and make an extended family holiday out of your honeymoon? *I don't think so!*

So your dad wants to do a funny slide show of your baby photos at the reception? *Thanks for your contribution!*

The purse strings holder

A mate of mine got married. He and his fiancée had just finished university and they were still living with their parents. So the parents together forked out a goodly sum for a traditional suburban middle-class wedding at a very nice restaurant-cum-wedding venue.

You can imagine my mate's surprise when he found out that of the 100 or so guests, almost 90 places had been 'bagsed' by the parents for their friends and relatives, many of whom were distant aunts and uncles from interstate and overseas, and some of whom my mate had never even heard of.

He and his fiancée were was less than impressed. They argued and appealed to their parents' sense of natural justice, but they didn't really have a leg to stand on, considering they had no money.

Sure, it's an extreme case, but the dilemma is universal. The person signing the cheque has, at the end of the day, a certain say in what goes on at your wedding. Just how much say they have depends on a subtle blend of them, you, negotiation, emotional blackmail and manipulation.

Hopefully they'll be gracious.

If not, maybe you'll just have to play hard-ball.

Personally, if my parents had said I could only have eight friends to my own wedding, I'd have called the whole thing off and had my own BYO barbie reception bash in the backyard... Well, actually, somebody else's backyard, cos my parents would've chucked me out.

Learning to negotiate

But your bow ties won't match the tablecloths ...
HUGH'S FIANCÉE

In Irving Berlin's great musical, *Annie Get Your Gun*, the two main characters, Annie Oakley and Frank Butler, sing a duet in which they discuss their plans for their upcoming wedding.

First, Frank serenades his fiancée and explains his ideas for the day. He wants a simple, old-fashioned family wedding with traditional vows in an old country chapel covered in orange blossoms.

While singing, Frank stares off into the middle distance with a whimsical expression, imagining the beautiful scene in his head. Unbeknown to him, however, Annie's expression gradually changes from affection to hostility. She clearly does not share the same vision as her soon-to-be.

Verse two kicks in, and she responds by saying that she wants a wedding with all the trimmings: ushers in fine suits, photographers, diamonds, bridesmaids and flower girls, a ceremony in a cathedral officiated by a bishop (but omitting the word 'obey' from the vows), followed by a reception in a five-star hotel with lots of caviar and champagne.

It's a recipe for disaster.

Mr Berlin was a perceptive observer of pre-marital negotiations. Sure, your fiancée and you will probably agree on most of the plans for your wedding, but it won't be a perfect match.

If you are fortunate, such discrepancies will be insignificant and entirely manageable:

She wants white napkins at the table. You like peach.

She wants 'Bohemian Rhapsody' for a processional. You prefer the Trumpet Voluntary.

She wants the groomsmen's bow ties to match the bridesmaid's lavender dresses. You want traditional black.

But what if, like Annie and Frank, the difference of ideas is more substantial? What if, for example:

She wants a civil ceremony with poetry and a song off a Beatles CD. You want to say your vows during a high-altitude world-record sky-diving attempt.

She wants to invite every person she's ever met to a fully-catered formal evening reception. You want an intimate lunch at your place.

She wants an eight-month overseas backpacking honeymoon. You want two weeks on a five-star cruiser.

Welcome to the world of marriage. This is your first hurdle, your trial by fire, your dive into the deep.

This is what it's all about.

This is marriage.

As a married couple, there'll be plenty of times when you don't see eye to eye, from everyday disagreements over superior washing-powder brands, through to almighty blues over whether or not you should move interstate.

So, as you start discussing plans and making inquiries and adding up prices, you'd better start working it out.

Listen to each other. Communicate your ideas clearly and calmly. Be realistic in terms of taste, logistics and costs. Negotiate. Sometimes, things won't go exactly how you want them to.

Constantly remind yourself that 'it's only a wedding' — a ceremony followed by a glorified party. There are millions of

Preparations

people in the world with much worse problems than whether or not the speeches should come *after* the cake or *before* it.

So go through all your planning with a positive attitude, a relaxed outlook, a flexible approach, a desire to get the job done and a willingness to compromise.

Except for one thing ...

Don't let your 14-year-old cousin and his rock band perform their debut gig for the after-dinner dancing.

Just trust me.

... your 14-year-old cousin and his rock band

Ker-ching! Ker-ching!

Everything about the word 'weddings' seems to prompt service providers to charge like the Light Brigade.

JANE FREEMAN

Have you heard the noise yet? *Swoosh* ... *ker-ching* ... *aaaggghhh!*

If you haven't already, don't worry. You will soon.

It is the sound of your wallet sliding out of your pocket (*swoosh*), being turned upside-down and emptied of all coinage, bills and credit cards (*ker-ching*), followed by your hysterical utterance as you punch numbers into a Wedding Planner Spreadsheet and total how much this whole thing is costing (*aaaggghhh!*).

What I'm saying is that your average suburban run-of-the-mill wedding is expensive. (Just ask the woman who in 1996 paid $40 000 for the wedding of ... wait for it ... her two cats! I kid you not.)

There are three reasons why weddings are expensive.

First, sheer bloody-minded profiteering on the part of all and sundry businesses and professionals within the wedding industry. These viper's brood, these blood-sucking freaks, these dog scrofula prey on poor romantic couples desperate to live out a fairytale.

Sure, everyone is entitled to make a living — do a job, get paid, put food on the table, take a good holiday, that sort of thing — and to be fair, there are heaps of photographers, florists, cake decorators, limo drivers, dressmakers, celebrants, musicians, restaurateurs and stationers who will give you a professional, straight-up service and a good product at a reasonable price.

But the other bastards, they smell you coming a mile off, and at the mere mention of the word 'wedding' their eyes flash up with dollar signs like in the cartoons and their prices miraculously receive a 'wedding levy' hike-up. To illustrate the point, in an article I read recently, an event organiser described how a car he organises for a corporate event is 50% of the price he is quoted for the same service with the word 'wedding' thrown in. (He explains that this is to make up for the fact that the mother-in-law will inevitable phone up 30 times to make sure everything is still okay.)

So as you go through all your preparations and plans and bookings, do your research.

Shop around.

Compare prices.

Explore alternatives.

Get brochures, prices and quotes, in the same way you would if you were pricing panel beating because some codger wearing a bowling hat took out your passenger door.

Make sure you know exactly what you get for your money. A wedding photographer might sound cheap, but later on you don't want to find out the hidden snag is that the quoted price was for time and skill only and 'oh-didn't-I-mention-that-the-prints-are-*extra*?'.

The second reason why a wedding can get expensive is *great expectations*.

Many couples have high hopes for their wedding day. Their ideas are the result of years of subconscious fantasy and mental note-taking at the weddings where they sat as guests. Or of sitting up in bed flicking through bridal magazines and getting sucked into the glamorous and oh-so-seductive prince-and-princess-for-a-day propaganda of lovely dresses, vintage cars, hairstyles, expensive diamonds and photo shoots on the sand, all of which cost dizzying sums.

Unfortunately, many of these extravagant ideas are driven more by romantic dreaming rather than the reality of the bank account. For some reason, when it comes to weddings, many normally astute and financially sensible adults lose their capability to make rational economic decisions. Clear-thinking managers of multi-nationals who make million-dollar decisions before breakfast become blithering idiots in the face of wedding negotiations, blindly forking out ten times the market value for a service or product. The fantasy meets with reality, but they pretend that the reality doesn't exist...which makes the reality a fantasy...which means that...Um...never mind.

It's like when I was a kid. Me and my mates would sit around discussing what sort of Porsche, BMW or Ferrari we would drive when we turned seventeen. My personal preference was for a Lotus that turned into a submarine like in that James Bond film. Then I turned seventeen ... and promptly bought a poxy second-hand station wagon with a billiard-ball gear stick and carpet in the back. The fantasy met with economic reality...and the fantasy lost.

So as you go through all your preparations and plans and bookings, be flexible about the kind of wedding you *can* and *should* afford. Be realistic about what constitutes value for money. Make good decisions.

By all means, have exciting dreams and hopes and plans, but view these in relation to the fact that someone has to pay for them, and be adaptable enough to modify some of your ideas.

For example, when a friend of mine got married recently, the quotes for the flowers (bridal bouquet, bouquets and buttonholes for attendants and parents, reception table arrangements) came in at over $1000.

This friend isn't stingy, but she couldn't come at the idea of spending so much money on flowers.

In the end, her sister went to the markets, bought the flowers for $200 and did the arranging herself, and nobody was the wiser. My friend had a few hundred bucks spare, which she put toward the honeymoon.

So work out which features of your wedding you want the most (i.e. imported lager at the reception), and which ones you can cut back on (i.e. a bridal dress. Surely she's got a nice frock in her cupboard?).

The third reason why expenses can sky-rocket is that you get caught off guard.

If you're not careful, wedding costs can quickly accumulate while you're not watching. You book a suit here and put a deposit on a venue there, buy a ring here and a dress there, organise a photographer here and pay for some plane tickets there, and on it goes. Each of these expenses in itself is not much of a burden... but bit by insidious bit, the total grows. Then the bills arrive.

It can happen so easily.

Like when I bought my aforementioned first car. I picked my station wagon up at a good price. But then I got talked into a stereo with four speakers and a graphic equaliser, reconditioned air, a rust spray and a once-in-a-lifetime deal of four new steel radials.

I figured, while I was paying that much money, a little bit more wouldn't matter. I almost signed for the lamb's wool seat covers before I realised I had added another 30% onto the car's original price and had blown my budget good and proper.

Jamie Packer did the same thing. For his wedding he spent $100 000 on flowers, $500 000 on tablecloths, lights and equipment, $150 000 on wedding cars, $250 000 on alcohol, $400 000 on food, $30 000 on a wedding dress, $4000 on a party dress, $350 000 on an engagement ring, $2 million on marquees, $2 million on getting Elton John, Jimmy Barnes and Human Nature to sing, $5 million on gold cufflinks and pendants for all 750 guests ... and before he knew it, he'd blown his $25 000 budget and was up around the $10 million mark.

So as you go through all your preparations and plans and bookings, have a budget and keep a close eye on it.

Whether you're wealthy or impoverished, whether you're having a quiet afternoon tea or a multi-million dollar society wedding, you still need to know ballpark figures for the kind of money you'll be shelling out.

Having said all this, I don't want to encourage you to be stingy. Your wedding day is special and it is appropriate to be extravagant on the celebrations. After all, it is (supposedly) a once-in-a-lifetime event. You want it to be special and classy and elaborate.

All I'm saying is, be sensible.

There's no point starting your married life in bankruptcy just because you thought it would be cute to have handmade Bavarian chocolates with your initials caramelised on the top.

The vortex

Inevitably, the lead-up to the nuptials will have driven you — as well as most of your family members and close personal friends — stark raving mad.

JANE FREEMAN

Getting married is a big deal.

What with all the plans and decisions and phone calls and discussions and dinner parties and champagne toasts and congratulatory emails, it's easy to be overwhelmed by it all.

And aside from preparing for one of the biggest and most expensive parties you're likely to have in your life, there's that other thing that comes afterwards; namely, a complete change in lifestyle, a significant redirection of the course of the remainder of your years, and commitment, sacrifice and monogamy.

Your wedding can become a production of epic proportion — a giant vortex which sweeps you in and tumbles you bum over pec until your whole purpose for existence seems to revolve around the 'big day'.

Everything else fades into oblivion, and before you know it you're waking at 4 am to debate the superiority of spinach roulade over choux puffs.

... until they become insane

I have spoken to plenty of wedding industry professionals who sigh and roll their eyes over the preciousness and intensity of some couples and their families. They describe brides reduced to hysterical sobbing during dress fittings; mothers who spend every weekend for eight months watching sample wedding videos; families brawling over floral colour schemes; and fathers who get abusive the moment the slightest detail doesn't go to plan.

That's a scary proposition for us guys, cos we're stuck right in the thick of it. So it's important in the months leading up to your wedding day that you (and your fiancée) occasionally step back, take a breath, have a look around and keep the whole thing in perspective.

Yes, your wedding is a big deal.

But no, it is not the single most important event in the history of mankind. There are plenty of people in the world with worse problems than the difficulty of deciding whether or not you should upgrade your honeymoon booking from the continental to the deluxe-breakfast package.

And at the very moment you say your all-important vows, there'll be billions of other people watching telly, going to work, reading comics while sitting on the toilet, cursing at red lights... and they are as oblivious to your existence as you are to theirs.

So don't get too precious about your wedding. Remember that while *your* world may be revolving around your marriage, the rest of the world is carrying on as usual. Have a look at a globe and notice that the entire city in which you live is only as big as the full-stop at the end of this sentence — that is, if it's there at all — and this will help to remind you of your place in the grand scheme of humanity.

And while I'm on a roll, I might also just mention this. Your friends and relatives will no doubt spend a few weeks celebrating with you. They will 'have you over' and talk a lot about your plans and who proposed to whom and where are you going to live and do you have any thoughts about the reception and by the way have *you* seen *our* wedding photos?

But they have their own lives to live.

Don't fall into the trap of thinking that your wedding is going to be the centrepiece of conversation for the next several months. There is nothing more boring than a couple who live under the misapprehension that their wedding is as important to everybody else as it is to them.

I have been to some shocker — repeat, *shocker* — dinner parties where the soon-to-be-married-couple at the end of the table fail to notice that the rest of us have now heard enough of their twee little pre-marital anecdotes. No matter what is said, the entire world relates in some way to their wedding. One of the dinner guests, Carrie, a stockbroker, is telling of how a business meeting went sour. She takes a sip of wine and continues, 'You just can't do that to a client! I vowed that if those scumbags ever set foot in my office again that...'

But she never gets to finish. Vince, the almost-married, chips in with, 'Speaking of vows, did you know that Sally and I are writing our own? Yes. We decided that the traditional *love, honour and obey* vows were too restrictive to fully express the depth of our love, so we...'

The assembled group gulps wine awkwardly.

And then, a few minutes later, Dave the dentist is telling the story about how he got a fine last week. Everybody is enthralled as he says, 'I couldn't believe it. So I get this ticket for going through a STOP sign. I mean, I'd *almost* stopped, not quite, you know, but the cop said that the car had to be completely stationary, so I said to him…'

'Speaking of *stationery*,' interrupts Sally the almost-married, 'Did you all know that our wedding invitations, name plates and thank-you cards are colour coordinated? Yes,' she leans in conspiratorially, 'Grey fleck with a gold embossing on 200 gsm card. It's the best money can buy.'

Boring.

So the next time a colleague says, 'How are the wedding plans coming along?' remember that they are just being polite.

Don't get out your personal organiser and give them a run-down on your wedding budget.

Just say, 'Fine,' and move on.

What's in a name?

What's in a name? That which we call a rose by any other name would smell as sweet ...

SHAKESPEARE, *ROMEO AND JULIET*

Before about AD 1000 in Europe, most people only had first names. With the exception of the most wealthy members of society, they were simply known as John or Phillip or Catherine or Susan or whatever.

Of course, the great flaw in this plan was that it was hard to distinguish one John from another.

'Morning, John.'

'Morning. How are you, John?'

'Fine thanks...Tell me, have you seen John today?'

'Yeah, he's up there talking to John.'

So by about AD 1400 (and thanks to the introduction of surnames on all legal documents), everyone had a surname.

Back then, people made up their own surnames, often based on their trade — i.e. Smith, Taylor, Cook, Baker, Hunter, Gardiner, Barber, Proctologist, Hooker — or whoever they were the son of — i.e. Jackson, Williamson, Johnson, Edmundson, Neilson, Dickson, Jamieson.

Surnames could also reflect a person's personality — i.e. Bright, Smiles, Goodman, Clownley, Love. (My own ancestors, the Downeys, must have been a gloomy bunch of beggars.) Or they could describe a person's physical characteristics — Armstrong, Little, Whitehead, Longfellow, Dick, Hardbutt. Or they could describe where a person lived — Westport, Castle, Hill, French, Slum.

Then, of course, there are those names the origins of which are best not thought about — Gump, Feeler, Schpitz, Washwell, Cowman, Cockburn.

After a while it became common practice for members of the same family to keep and use the same surname.

In previous patriarchal centuries, when a woman married a man she left her own family and joined her husband's, and in doing so adopted his surname. The post-feminist world of the twenty-first century, however, has seen the evolution of the cult of the individual. Rather than a woman joining a man's family, most couples now view their marriage as two people joining together equally to start a *new* family. So it is now no longer assumed that a woman at marriage will take her husband's name.

As you approach your marriage, your fiancée and you will probably at some point discuss this name thing.

My advice to you is this: take it in your stride. It's no big deal.

If your wife wants to take your surname, fine. (My wife took mine, and so did most of our middle-class suburban married friends. It's traditional, and it saves a lot of hassle when you're trying to open new bank accounts.)

If your wife wants to keep her surname, that's fine too. We don't live in a male-dominated world any more. You and your wife are partners in this marriage venture. You wouldn't even consider changing *your* name to *hers*, would you? Didn't think so. Now you know how she feels.

Interesting days lie ahead in the surname stakes.

We are now seeing the emergence of a new generation of surnames; for the first time in history these are the children of parents with different surnames. They are kids with names like Clarke-Smith, Diver-Brown, Winfield-McDonald and Village-Idiot.

What perplexes me is what will happen when *this* generation grows up, marries and has children of its own. What will happen, for example, when a Benson-Packer marries and has a child with a Kent-Michaels? Is the next generation likely to be littered with names like McConnaugh-Smith-O'Neill-Pederson and Buckle-Power-Reading-Gently?

Or will they chop up bits of their names to invent totally new ones, like Smithsonbumhopper or Copyadinglejohanbaum?

Only time will tell... but my earnest hope is that the children of the next generation won't end up with names like the famous British major of World War I, commonly known as Leone Sextus Denys Oswolf Fraduati Tollemache-Tollemache-de Orellana-Plantaganet-Tollemache-Tollemache.

But it's tradition ...

Traditions have one purpose. To be broken.
MAE WEST

All around the world, every hour of every day of every year, people are getting married.

From the streets of Sydney to the lanes of London, from the top of Tamworth to the bottom of Bumbu, from the valleys of Vroomshoop to the shores of San Francisco, from the steppes of Shiting to the snowdrifts of Stupsk, from the volcanic vents of Volgogradskoje to the tundra of Taan, from the prettily peppered purple plateaus of Pleasantville to the marvellously manicured mellow mountains of Montreal, every hour of every day of every year, people are getting married.

And despite the immense differences in culture and kilometres, these weddings all have the same three components.

First, there's some sort of courting period, ranging from having the bride picked for you at age three, to living with someone for ten years.

Then there's the ceremony, witnessed by others and performed by someone with the legal authority to do so (priest, celebrant, witchdoctor, elder, rabbi, Captain Picard).

Finally there's the celebration attended by family and friends, whether it be champagne toasts at the local bowling club, or sitting around a fire drinking goat's blood out of a coconut.

As you start to 'create' your wedding day, there are literally hundreds of decisions that will shape the tone and style and timing and feel of the day.

This is important stuff, so if you're reading this late at night in bed and your breathing is heavy and your eyes are doing that droopy thing, SNAP OUT OF IT AND PAY ATTENTION!

Right.

As you start making all these earth-shattering decisions, there is one element that you must grasp.

A majority of what happens at weddings has absolutely nothing to do with legal requirements. Technically speaking, at its bare bones, after giving adequate notice you could go to a registry office wearing a pair of overalls covered in compost with your bride in a swimsuit and sunhat, both say 'I want to marry him/her', sign a bit of paper in front of a couple of witnesses, write a cheque and walk out a few minutes later as husband and wife.

Think about this for a moment.

No, really, I mean it.

A lot of the activity surrounding weddings is not necessary. Nice, yes. Fun, yes. 'Romantic', yes. But not legally necessary. It is purely, solely, wholly and utterly done for one reason ... *tradition*.

In organising a wedding, most couples simply imitate what they've seen at every other wedding they've been to ... the same cars, the same suits, the same poses in front of sunsets, the same acoustic guitar songs during the signing of the papers, the same menu, the same speeches, the same white three-tiered wedding cake, the same awkward waltz, the same cans strung up behind their car filled with balloons and confetti, the same...the same...the same...

Not that there's anything *wrong* with any of these things. Some traditions serve a purpose. For example, you don't *have to* have speeches at your wedding, but it's appropriate to thank a handful of relevant people and say a few words of appreciation and farewell.

All I'm saying is that it's your wedding and you should *decide* on the various features of the day, rather than just *inheriting* them by default.

So, assuming that you can do it without World War III, start your wedding plans with a blank sheet of paper. As Jane Freeman wrote of modern weddings in her article 'White Mischief', 'all the old rules have gone out the window.'

Create your wedding from the ground up. For every decision you make, ask yourself *why?*

Church or garden or seaside service? Attendants? Professional photographer? Hired suits? Flowers? Limousines? Traditional vows? Telegrams? A little plastic bride and groom sitting atop a white cake? Dancing?

I have been to plenty of weddings which broke from tradition: a wedding in a school hall; a wedding where the bride and groom arrived together; a wedding where the bride wore a nice tailored outfit rather than a cream puff; a wedding with no photo or video; a wedding where the official vehicles were VW-convertibles, not limos; a wedding where anyone could take the mike and say a few words; a wedding where the guests all 'brought a plate'; a wedding with no reception; and a couple who didn't have rings. I have even heard of (get ready for it) brides with blokes as 'bridesmaids' and blokes with women as 'best men'. (Years from now, people will read this and think, 'Oh, how passé,' but on the Sunday afternoon I'm writing this, it is still pretty 'wow!')

Together with your bride, make your own decisions and custom-design your wedding day. (Sure, you'll probably end up doing lots of traditional stuff anyway. I just know you're salivating at the prospect of drinking a cold ale in the back of a '43 chauffeured Rolls.)

One of the great freedoms you have is that the 'new tradition' is to break from old tradition. Couples today are less frightened of doing their own thing, like wearing a safari suit instead of a tux, or having a big party with modern music instead of a formal bash with eighteenth-century waltzes. Many women are now keeping their surnames instead of becoming 'Mrs Jones née Miss Julie Smith'.

Unfortunately, breaking with tradition won't go down too well with your mum, who will insist that Uncle Kev has to be the MC because he is at all family functions. *'His Winston Churchill impersonation is a cracker!'* she'll chortle.

If people keep pushing 'tradition' on you, tell them you've decided to adopt the ancient tradition of the Aztecs, who sacrificed the bride's family's first-born son and ate his liver over their wedding altar, or the tradition of the Oopi-Oohamboss, who spend their first night as husband and wife having sex in a smoky tent watched by all the old women of the families.

That'll shut them up.

4
Practicalities

(someone has to organise it)

'When my best man got married, he organised their wedding in about two weeks. We were the opposite. If anyone tells you organising a wedding is easy, they're a pathological liar.

Samantha's mum started with a folder with about 50 menus in it, and we had to go through each one and calculate how many bacon bagels and glasses of champagne each guest would have. There were so many different permutations, depending on where we had the reception and how many guests we invited. Countless nights were spent discussing cakes and hire cars and floral arrangements. I'm just glad I had nothing to do with the dress.

'The only thing we didn't fuss over was the ceremony. The Rev ran through it with us and we both said, "Great, that's for us!"'

ARN, 22

Timing, timing ...

I don't know what all the fuss was about. I thought a midnight wedding was a novel idea.

JACQUES

One of your first decisions will be the timing of your wedding.

Without a shadow of a doubt, every single person to whom you say 'Vicki and I are getting married' will ask you the same question. No matter how far you travel or who you tell, the question is always the same:

'*When?*'

The choice for us was easy. Meredith had just finished uni and I was a teacher, so we got married on Day One of the summer holidays.

But many couples — unless they've done considerable spadework before they announce — have only a vague idea of 'when'. The response will usually be something like, 'At the end of the year' or 'When Mitch can get holidays' or 'That depends on Janet's parole officer' or even 'We haven't even talked about it yet.'

Eventually, you have to choose a date.

The timing of your wedding depends on a number of factors.

Your concept of 'engagement'
The word 'engagement' literally refers to the period in which you are under promise to be wed. It is the time between 'Will you marry me?' and 'I take this woman'.

Some couples live in a permanent state of engagement with no real idea of when they're going to get married. The current world record belongs to the 82-year-old fiancées who got married in Mexico ... after a 67-year engagement! Personally, I don't see the point of the semi-eternal engagement. It's like saying you're going on a holiday ... and then waiting in the departure lounge at the airport for five years.

Once you decide to get married, why muck about?

Just set a date and do it.

At the opposite extreme (for example, in Vegas), some engagements last from the time it takes to get from the roulette wheel to the drive-through Elvis chapel. (This is approximately 19 minutes — coincidentally, the same length of time I would expect such a marriage to last.)

Based on personal observation, it seems to me that most couples are engaged for about six to twelve months. Without dragging on too long, this gives them enough time to settle in to the idea, work through a few issues, make preparations, maybe set up a new domicile, put a few extra bucks away for miscellaneous costs and plan their wedding ceremony and an enormous party.

Friends of mine went from proposal to the altar in nine weeks and they reckon that was plenty of time to organise everything.

Personal calendars
Getting married takes time. You'll need time before your wedding day to deal with the infinite last-minute arrangements.

You'll need a clear day on which to get married.

And you'll need a few weeks to recover, celebrate and relax together afterwards in some love den with a heart-shaped spa and an extended cocktail hour.

Get out your calendars, diaries and palm pilots and find a time when you and your bride can pull holidays, or at least find a time when work is not too busy. Avoid major deadlines, meetings, events, interviews and tiny gaps between overseas or interstate trips.

Let your employers and clients know your plans so they can make their own arrangements too.

If you're studying, be cautious. I know a guy who failed a final uni exam and had to re-sit the paper. But the exam was scheduled bang in the middle of his honeymoon. He sorted it out, but it took a lot of doing.

Once you've set the day, use a big red felt marker to scribble out a huge block around it on your calendar. Don't book anything anywhere near that time.

I've said it before, I know, but let me say it again: when you get married, there's a lot to do. You have to get used to your new relationship and role and at the same time try to finalise the last-minute details and organise the biggest party you'll ever host. You'll also have to plan an enormous holiday honeymoon and, simultaneously maybe, set up a home, buy furniture and electricals, organise a mortgage, change your wills and, if you're really lucky, cope with a change of job or an interstate move.

At any other time, any *one* of these things would in isolation be a big hassle. Have you ever moved house or shopped around for a new bed? Combine these activities and mix in for good measure the nervous tension and emotional investment, and you've got a cocktail for disaster.

So give yourself plenty of space to get it all done.

Guests

Recently, Meredith and I tried to organise a dinner with two other couples. The days of back 'n' forth phone calls that ensued trying to get a date when everyone was free was nothing short of a telephonic comedy of errors.

Our simple meal for a table of six was eventually booked...11 weeks away! Extrapolating using basic mathematical principles, a wedding for 150 guests would need to be booked five years in advance.

Problem: It's impossible to pick a date that will suit everyone on your guest list.

Solution: Don't pick a date that will suit everyone on your guest list.

Some of your guests won't be able to come to your wedding, and they'll just have to miss out. It's their bad luck, although it actually works in your favour because you can then invite others from the 'B' list. (But don't tell them that.)

Run a few dates past your most key, inner-circle, VIP family and friends — you know, the people who absolutely have to be there (the mums, dads, special uncles and aunts, siblings, closest friends, your ex-girlfriends) — and pick a date. The others can take their chances.

When your mum starts making a fuss and wanting your wedding postponed for another six months so that your Aunt Edna can recover from her varicose vein operation, tell her you'll post Aunt Edna the video.

Availability of venues

At this very moment there are scores of other people just like you, sitting around a dining-room table making preparations for their wedding day. Some of them are planning to be married at the same time on the same day as you. (They'll be the ecstatic couples with shiny wedding bands who you'll inevitably meet at the trivia night on your honeymoon.)

So if you have ideas, hopes or fixations for a particular church or reception venue, you best get cracking. Because while you're sitting up in bed reading this book, those other couples are there right now discussing menus and paying deposits.

This is a chicken and egg scenario.

Do you find out when your ideal wedding and reception venue are available, and then declare *that* as your wedding day?

Or do you pick a day and then search for places that are available?

It's up to you (and the other key players) and how hung up you are on going to a specific place like an old stone chapel, waterfront restaurant or vineyard.

Personally, I wouldn't muck about too much. The important thing is that you get married, not that you have this church because it has amazing stained glass or that garden because the flowers will be in full bloom.

Once-in-a-blue-moon events

Nine-hundred and ninety-nine times out of a thousand, this factor won't even come into consideration.

But if your wedding day is the one unlucky one in the thousand, it could be disastrous.

What I'm talking about are the major community functions, festivals or events taking place in the vicinity of your wedding venue. Various roads or parts of your town or locality could virtually shut down on a specific day because of a parade, sporting event or public ceremony. Transport could be a problem.

For example, if you want to get married in the little chapel next door to the Olympic Stadium on the same day as the Opening Ceremony of the games, leave ten hours to get between the church and the reception venue.

Honeymoon

While I don't want to suggest that your marriage revolves around a post-wedding holiday, it again boils down to how hung-up you are about a particular destination.

I know a couple who set their wedding back several months because they were determined to have their honeymoon in the place where they first met — a ski lodge. So they waited till winter. The opposite applies if you're desperate for the sun'n'surf-resort thing in summer.

Another factor to consider is the possible impact of school holidays on your honeymoon, when literally thousands of frenzied families are unleashed upon the roads, airlines, resorts, camping areas and other miscellaneous holiday destinations. You may fantasise about a leisurely and quiet drive to a coastal resort where you will enjoy cocktails by the pool as the sun sets, only in reality to find the roads clogged with station wagons laden with bicycles and the pool over-run with screaming tykes who keep nailing you in the head with a volleyball.

Not exactly the stuff of romantic fantasy.

In addition, keep in mind that school holidays are peak times for travel and accommodation costs, so you'll be paying top dollars if you honeymoon at such times.

⤺

There are many inconvenient hurdles on the road to choosing your wedding day. Don't baulk...just jump over them.

Work through the issues and hopefully you'll soon have a day with a very special asterisk marked against it on your calendar.

Get used to that date.

Remember it.

Remember it well.

Have it tattooed on your scrotum, if necessary.

Because once a year you will have to remember this date and celebrate it...and if you ever forget it, there'll be hell to pay.

Once you've got a date sorted out, you then need to turn your attention to timing on the day itself.

You may opt for a late-morning wedding and lunch if you are doing some driving afterwards or if you have a plane, train or boat to catch. Or you may prefer a late-afternoon wedding to free up the morning to go for a surf or play some golf with a few mates.

Other factors may come into play...like a long-standing desire to have wedding photos in the midday sun on the beach, or a sunset cruise. There's nothing to stop you having an early morning wedding and brunch...oh, except that all the females would need to start getting their hair and make-up done at 3 am. And that's just not fair.

The timing of the day's events needs to be worked out with military precision. The scope of some weddings makes the invasion of Normandy look like a simple boating afternoon.

Create a schedule of all the events of the day. For example, transport to the wedding venue, length of the service (add 15 minutes minimum for bridal lateness), chatting afterwards, brief photo shoot, transport to the reception venue, meeting people and mingling at the reception, meal service (and the consumption thereof), speeches, cake cutting, dancing, hanging loose at the end, miscellaneous photography, lengthy farewells to the bride's friends who didn't make the cut into the bridal party and who choose midnight to have a special moment with her, transport outa there, and so.

Remember that no matter how carefully you plan, everything will take much longer than you expect, so add 10% to all your calculations. It's better to have a bit of time up your sleeve than to run ragged all day.

Guest list

We were having a reception for 140 guests. Our first-draft guest list hit 320. We hadn't even started and already we were in trouble.

TED W. PEENROY

Here's a little story. You'll get the point as you go along.

The scene: You and your fiancée are in a lifeboat in the middle of the ocean. Swimming around you in the freezing, shark-infested waters are all your family members and friends... and you, as captains of the lifeboat, get to pick who gets in.

There are 60 seats in the lifeboat, but the problem is, there are 200 people in the water.

What would you do?

You'd be forced to put a value on people and weigh them up in relation to others. You'd have to choose who to save and, by a process of negation, who to leave in the briny.

Imagine the scene as you and your fiancée stood at the bow, calling out the names of those lucky enough to get in.

'Okay, first, both our mums and dads,' you call as they haul themselves up over the side. 'And our brothers and sisters.'

'And their wives and husbands too,' pipes up your fiancée as you scan the bobbing heads in the water.

'Yeah, and their kids. Right ... how many seats have we got left?'

'Forty-five.'

'Right ... Ted and Alice, Aunty Julie, Jane, Mick ...'

'Pssst,' your fiancée whispers, 'how many kids have Steve and Jean got?'

'Ah ... seven I think,' you reply conspiratorially.

'Too many! We'll leave them, then?'

'Yeah.'

'Right, let's see now ... Bob, Martina, Gustav ...'

'Julie from the netball team ...'

'No! If we let her in, we have to let them all in ...'

'All right, well Margie ... Mario and his girlfriend ...'

'No, not his girlfriend, we hardly know her ...'

The little boat suddenly lurches dangerously to starboard. You look over in horror to see a multitude of strangers pulling themselves in.

'What the hell's going on?' you yell.

Your fiancée's mum gives you a wave from the stern. 'It's all right, dear, I've invited our relatives and old family friends to join us. Some of them knew Lucy when she was just a sparkle in her father's eyes. There are only 50 of them ...'

'But ... but ...' you sputter, 'but the boat's almost full!'

'Oh no, dear,' she replies, her voice adopting the timbre of brittle china, 'there'll be plenty of room. This is actually *my* lifeboat. All *your* friends have to get back in the water.'

This is exactly what it's like deciding who to invite to your wedding. The organisation of your guest list might very well be the longest and single most horrendous experience of your entire life.

There are three reasons for this:

1. You may have to juggle a nightmare web of relational politics. If your family and friendship group has splits, divisions

and divorces in the ranks, or friends not on speaking terms or relatives who can't be in the same room at the same time, then you'll probably face some resistance to your plan to have them all under the one roof smiling sweetly in a photograph together.

For example, a friend of mine's mother said that if he invited his dad (her ex-husband) to their wedding, she wouldn't be there. To add salt to the wound, his sister then said if their dad *wasn't* there, *she* wouldn't be going.

You will have to draw on your subtle skills of negotiation, persuasion and people management. You might even have to face the tough decision of not inviting one person or group out of deference for another.

Personally, I find this idea abhorrent. I know that relationships are complex, but surely any adult can cope with a few hours for a wedding? Invite whoever you want. Put the ball in their court and let them work out if they have a problem. If they don't come, it's their decision.

2. It forces you to place a monetary value on your relationships. The maths works like this:

a) You have a certain amount to spend on your wedding. Let us call this V dollars.

b) Each person invited to your wedding will cost a set sum. Let us call this Y dollars.

c) There are a number of people who you and your fiancée want to be at your wedding. Let us call this figure Z.

d) There are a number of people who you and your fiancée don't necessarily want to be at your wedding, but your parents do. Let us call this figure W.

Putting it all together:

If $(Z+W) \times Y > V$, then you're in trouble.

You will have to reduce Z, or tell some of your W to POQ, or find a place with a cheaper Y until you're under V.

In the real world, this boils down to some tough decisions.

Sure, you may like Phil from the office, but do you like him enough to spend a horrendous sum to fill him and his girlfriend with baked gorgonzola and pear tartlets washed down with Brut N/V at your reception?

3. The different key players in your wedding have their own mental lists of who they want to invite.

This is fine... so long as everyone agrees.

But when they don't, there is potential for family discord of epic proportion, with conflicts falling anywhere on the scale between awkward differences of opinion to major rifts that split entire families for years at a time.

If you're paying for your own wedding, this probably won't be an issue. You and your fiancée can invite whoever you want to invite, and that's that. But even in this scenario, don't be surprised if Mum or Dad put on the thumbscrews about how your second cousin Eddie would just be devastated if he wasn't invited, even though you haven't seen him since you were ripping legs of insects as five-year-olds.

However, if you are not bearing the financial burden of the wedding, you're at the mercy of whoever's holding the chequebook — probably Mum and Dad — and you can bet they've got some firm ideas about the guest list.

When some friends of mine got married, both their sets of parents clogged up the wedding list with ancient friends of the family and relatives they didn't even know they had until they looked them up in the family trees. There was no room left for the bride and groom's friends — which naturally led to much division in the marital camp, with the word 'elopement' even making a guest appearance during one heated discussion.

I know another couple who had quite a struggle resolving their guest list. The groom's wealthy parents expected an enormous gala wedding with an equally enormous guest list. The bride's working-class parents wanted a simple affair with a small guest list. The groom's parents said they would pay. The bride's parents were insulted. The ensuing negotiations were awkward and tense.

Practicalities

Okay, enough horror stories.

After you've worked through the family politics and power stratas, you will have to put pen to paper and write your guest list.

This is no easy task.

In theory, both families should be evenly represented and able to invite a number of friends and relatives, regardless of who's paying. And it goes without saying that you and your bride should also be able to invite a number of your own friends.

When it came time for me and Meredith to write our guest list, we filled an entire notepad with names. We had friends from school, church and uni, work colleagues, acquaintances from a number of clubs, teams and groups as well as extensive multi-generational relative networks and huge numbers of friends of our parents who had known us since we were lumps on the other side of a maternity dress.

The list was nothing short of enormous.

Even when we cut the 'dead wood' (no offence, guys) from the list, the cost of an 'average wedding' was still staggering. Which

... nutting out the guest list

led to an interesting choice: for roughly the same price, either we could have a *quarter* the people on our list for a three course sit-down reception, or we could have *all* the people on our list for a fully catered afternoon tea.

After much debate, we opted for the latter, on the basis that people are more important than entrées and tablecloths. It was a decision we did not regret. And we were fortunate that our parents were easygoing and didn't have any inflexible romantic notions about the reception.

Many friends of ours have gone through nights of torment trying to work out who to invite and who not to invite. Your turn will come too. You will soon be having discussions with all the subtlety of an old-style slave auction as you chat over the pros and cons of your guests like you're talking to your butcher about various cuts of meat.

You will find yourself in the ludicrous situation of weighing up the merits of cousin Frank and when was the last time you saw him and how much time have you spent with him during your life and how does he stand in relation to Naomi, the new woman at work whom you've only known for six months but get on well with and know you'll be working together for a while... And then there's Justine from uni who you hung out with for four years but who you don't really see any more, to say nothing of Tony from school, but if you invite Tony then you have to invite Robert, Lan, Gail and Melissa, all of whom are married, but you don't know their husbands and wives very well.

Your floor will end up covered with pages of names pencilled in, scribbled out, screwed up, started again ... You will spend nights in circular discussions with your fiancée, writing and rewriting lists.

If you're having trouble trying to nut out your guest list, you may find it useful to draw up a large 'archery target' design. Fill in the names of the most important guests (mums, dads, bridal party) in the bulls-eye. Then move outwards till the you get to the outer circle where you put the relatives you've never met and friends you haven't spoken to in years. Then work out where the 'cut' is to be made.

If this method doesn't work and you're still having problems with your guest list — perhaps because you need to reduce it by 20% but you have already hit the absolutely uncuttable barrier — try some of these ideas:

1. Change to a cheaper or bigger reception venue. This may require a radical re-think of your plans for the day.
2. Have an inconvenient reception that most people won't come to, for example, on Christmas morning, or on the top of a granite pinnacle that requires a 400 metre vertical rock-climb to get to. Or have a 'nude reception'.
3. Elope.
4. Send your invitations out so late that half your guests receive them the day before your wedding.
5. Hold your wedding at the same time as a big work conference when all your colleagues will be out of town, or at the same time as a relative's wedding so that they soak up all the family dead wood. (Remember, it doesn't matter whether they come or not, it's the fact that you *invited* them that counts.)
6. Be ruthless. I recently read an article that ran through the arrangements and details of about 50 celebrity weddings of famous politicians, musicians, media people, sports stars and business people around the world. While there were some biggies (400–750 guests), most of them had between 75 and 150 guests. You don't need to invite everyone you've ever met in your life.

One final word. When you've finished your 'archery target' of names, burn it. Nothing sours a friendship more than if visiting friends stumble across your list in the recycling bin and discover that they're in the outer circle along with your kindy teacher, the milkman and the guy who coached your soccer team when you were seven.

Invitations

Your wedding invitations should be one of the most important aspects of your planning. You must spend a lot of time and effort getting them just right. They will set the tone for your special day and it is imperative that they match your other stationery.

GUY RASSAN, WEDDING EXPERT

Stop.
See that quote up there?
It's a typical example of stupid mindless crap that wedding books love to espouse.
Let's keep this all in perspective, shall we?
An invitation is just that: an invitation. A nice piece of paper that says, 'We're getting married at this place at this time. Do you wanna come?'
That's all.
Don't get too precious about your invitations. Yes, make them nice, but don't get silly.

Content

A formal invitation should say:

- *Who the invite is from.*

Your guests need to know who to respond to. The invite comes from the hosts, who are usually the people slapping down the plastic (you, your parents, the bride's parents, or some twisted family tree combination of parents, single parents, divorced parents and step-parents).

- *Who the invite is to.*

This is very important, particularly if you are having an expensive reception and you really want to make it clear that while you're keen for Uncle George and Aunty Joan to attend, they're kidding themselves if they think you're going to pay a few hundred bucks for their seven kids to have a couple of glasses of lemonade, a plate of smoked salmon and bit of wedding cake.

- *Who is getting married.*

Der.

- *Where the ceremony is taking place.*

If getting married in a church, usually the name and suburb will suffice. If at a wedding venue, garden, house or hall, the address should be included as well.

- *When the marriage service is taking place.*

Day, date, month and year... and don't forget what time.

- *Where the reception is taking place.*

Include the name of the venue, as well as the address. If it's in a home, specify whose it is.

- *The dress code.*

Your guests need to know the style of your wedding so they can dress appropriately. You need to tell them if it's black-tie, formal, informal, casual, fancy dress, etc. I was once invited to a wedding where we were asked to wear a 'lounge suite', which as you can imagine presented some logistical problems.

- *RSVP details.*

Formal invitations give a reply address, as protocol dictates that a written invitation requires a written response. You may also include a name and telephone number, but make sure you've got a good answering machine or a reliable person to take the calls. You don't want your seven-year-old brother saying, 'When you were out, three people phoned and said they were coming to your wedding... but I don't remember who they were.'

- *RSVP date.*

Set it about two or three weeks before D-Day, to allow follow-up on all the slackers who are late with some pathetic excuse about how they've been meaning to respond but the invite got caught in a pile of papers on the kitchen corkboard. Check also with your reception venue or caterers for the date by which they need definite numbers.

Wording

The wording of a wedding invitation is a reflection of the style of the wedding.

If it's an over-the-top black-tie affair and the invitations are individually gold embossed, the wording will be quite formal.

If it's a backyard barbie kind of reception, written on 'We're having a party!' stationery, then the phrasing will be colloquial.

Here's a few examples of the style and wording often used in invitations. Tailor these to your own taste and situation.

A traditional formal invitation from the bride's parents goes something like this:

Mr David and Dr Julianne Wauchope
request the pleasure of the company of
Jack and Jill Montgomery
at the marriage of their daughter
Susan Eliza
to Mr Benjamin Gumpenshtievel
at St Pauls Church, Thrillby-on-Waterford
on Saturday 10th December, 2005
at 3 o'clock

*and afterwards at Big Jugs Family Restaurant
128 Brighton Street, Stanfield.
RSVP
15th November, 2005
210 Headland Road, Rochester, 3576
DRESS: Black-tie*

You may, however, choose to be more informal:

*Hymie Rosenthal and Cindy Hotlever
will be married
on Sunday, 14th March 2005
at 2 pm
at the Hotlever home
17 Dresden Drive, Newport.
This will be followed by an afternoon tea in the garden.
We would be delighted if you could join us.
RSVP ...*

If you wanted to be even more informal, you could handwrite or print a prose-style invitation:

*Dear Jillian
We are getting married at 10 am on Sunday 27th March on the sand at Apostle Beach, Maryborough. We hope you can join us to celebrate our wedding.
We'll be putting on a picnic lunch afterwards, so it would be great if you could let us know by 1st March if you'll be there.
Love,
Geoff and Christine
P.S. Apostle Beach is a nudist beach.*

Production

If you want your invitations to be printed professionally, check out your local wedding stationers and small printing firms who are less likely to charge through the nose.

Most of these businesses have standard wedding print packs and plenty of professional advice.

The rest is up to your taste and budget. You can do your invites on normal paper, thicker water-marked paper, stone tablet, coloured stock, patterned stock, light card, cowhide, embossed card, toilet paper, translucent waxed paper. Font styles and ink colours are equally wide-ranging. Then there's the bits like borders, flourishy squiggles, hearts and cupids icons, special folds and ribbon-ties, wax seals and an abundance of other stuff beyond my comprehension.

Make sure you know exactly what is included in the printer's costs.

And make sure that if you want matching stationery for all the other bits and pieces (envelopes, place cards, thankyou notes, order of service) the paper stock is available, and not going to cost you ridiculous prices.

Many couples produce their own invitations. These are certainly cheaper, and with a decent computer and a touch of artistic ability, not necessarily lacking in quality.

For our wedding, Meredith's cousin, who is an artist, hand-painted all the stationery with flower motifs (my suggestion for a monster-truck motif was quickly rejected) and individually hand-calligraphed all the names.

I have received some memorable invites with the home-made touch:

- An art-print postcard from a gallery with the invitation hand-written on the back.
- A colour collage of photos of the couple with the words written around the border.
- An invitation on card cut into jigsaw-puzzle pieces. This was memorable, although ultimately annoying and self-indulgent.
- A photograph with the wording of the invitation written in lipstick across a pair of enormous breasts. (Nice one, Jim.)

Other info

Aside from the invitation, it may be appropriate to send out other information. If any of the venues are difficult to find, or if it's an 'out of town' wedding, a sketched or photocopied map may be useful. If appropriate, guests may appreciate the contact details of local hotels, motels and guesthouses.

Some couples include a 'gift registry' card. This points them to a personalised list kept at a specific department store which details all the stuff they'd like as presents.

I can see why some people use a gift registry. It means that they can target the stuff they need and want for their new life, thereby avoiding the possibility of getting 11 breadboards and 16 sets of drink coasters. And it gives them the opportunity to be given something they wouldn't normally get, like a mate of mine who listed a home-brew kit and computer-golf software.

However, I have to say that I'm not in favour of the gift registry. It rings a little mercenary for my liking, especially when you have people like Prince Edward and Sophie putting on their registry a $94 000 cutlery set. (Fortunately for me, I RSVPd 'no' to their wedding.) According to the strict rules of etiquette, one should never presume to be getting a gift. It should come 'from the heart'. Writing a list takes some of the creativity, spontaneity and surprise out of the equation. It also implies that any gift not listed on the registry is somehow inferior or unwanted.

Maybe I've just had too many bad experiences. Every time I've checked a register, I've discovered that the pepper mill, doorstop and bookends have already gone and I'm stuck with a choice between a portable phone, a ride-on lawn mower or a microwave oven.

At which point I purchase scented soaps.

What to wear?

Dress like a million bucks ...
for a fraction of the cost.

SIGN OUTSIDE SUIT-HIRE SHOP

I'm going to keep this real short, because fashion isn't really my thing. And I abhor those cheesy bridal magazines and their 'Dress to Impress — Sensational wedding day wear for that special man' features.

Also, I don't think you're an idiot.

What you wear on your wedding day will reflect your personality and the style of your wedding. Most ordinary suburban blokes having ordinary suburban weddings get married in something fairly formal to match the import of the occasion, like a suit, a kilt, ceremonial mau-mau or a kaftan.

It is common practice for the attendants (best man plus any number of groomsmen) to wear outfits that match the groom's, although this is just one of those aesthetic traditions that ultimately has no basis, except maybe to look good in wedding photos.

You may want to buy a new suit for your wedding. If you can get your groomsmen to invest in new suits, fine, although it's a bit of an ask for just one day. Many blokes wear their own suits, and if they don't match, they at least wear matching shirts or ties.

If you're set on the clone thing, you'll probably have to rent. Go somewhere good that has quality suits that don't smell funny. Suit fashions change, so make sure the suits you get are not 20-year-old throwbacks. You don't want to end up in a polyester safari suit that makes you look like a bad nightclub singer. And keep an eye open for cheap material, frayed seams or shiny and worn elbow patches that are like a neon sign above the wearer's head declaring to all and sundry: 'Cheap suit-cheap guy'.

The traditional suit, of course, is black. It looks smart and is less likely to date than other colours. But depending on the style of your wedding, anything can go. Rocker Tommy-Lee Jones got married the first time in a pair of black jeans on the beach, and the second time in the nude. Cindy Crawford's husband Randy also got married on a beach. Looking like a throwback from a cigarette commercial, he wore bare feet, black pants and an untucked, unbuttoned white shirt. Custard lead-singer David McCormick recently got married in a $40 op-shop suit — to match his bride's PVC nurse's outfit with knee-length leather boots, one can only surmise.

I know one couple who for their garden wedding dressed as Julie Andrews and Dick Van Dyke from the 'Supercalifragilisticexpialidocious' sequence in Mary Poppins. He wore white pants, white shoes, a lollypop stripe jacket, boater, bow tie and cane. Sure, he looked ridiculous, but he enjoyed himself, and that's the main thing.

Take care also with accessories. Have a good pair of shoes, which according to many style professionals is the most important element of any outfit. Bright red socks with your name embroidered on them are definitely not on. Think too about tiepins, stickpins, cufflinks, kerchiefs and a brand new pair of black silk boxer shorts.

Basically, when you stand up there, you want to feel damn fine and look damn good.

When it comes to choosing the style of your clothes, I'd suggest the following:

- Don't look at photos of grooms in bridal magazines, because those guys are models and you're not. They have make-up artists and consultants and designers and stylists and professional photographers and managers, and they could wear an outfit made of bananas and still make it look cool. You couldn't.
- Don't choose anything too trendy or extreme. The more fashionable you are, the more *un*fashionable your photos will eventually become. Just ask my mate who got married in the eighties in a Sergeant Peppers outfit with (wait for it) one glove. At the time, he thought he was cutting-edge. But now he keeps his wedding photos under lock and key.
- Let your fiancée have no say in what you and your attendants wear. Wear something that will suit the style and formality of the wedding, but don't get into any of that bow ties-matching-the-bridesmaids'-dresses crap. What are you? A man or a fashion accessory? If she persists, tell her you want her bridesmaids to wear black leather to match your groomsmen's belts.
- Wear something special and comfortable that makes you feel and look good. For some bizarre reason, guys about to get married lose their common sense and suddenly think that it's a good idea to wear white tie, tails and a top hat in the middle of summer. You don't have to wear funky pinstripe grey with weird vests and cummerbunds, either. You don't want to spend the whole day feeling that everybody's giggling behind your back.

In short, wear something that suits you and makes you feel relaxed. However, if you're going to dress as Spartacus, at least do your bride the courtesy of telling her beforehand. You don't want her fainting halfway down the aisle.

Music

If music be the food of love, play on.
WILL SHAKESPEARE

The food of love — music — 'makes a beautiful accompaniment to your perfect day'.

Or so say the ads.

There's something about a stirring hymn or a moving melody that adds dignity and class to a wedding day. It sets the tone and complements the significance of the occasion. I'm a bit of a muso myself, so music was very important to me at my wedding. We had an organ processional, recessional and hymns during the service, duelling flutes during the signing of the register and our favourite songs during the reception.

The music you choose to punctuate your wedding day is dependent upon four factors:

1. Your budget (if you're strapped for cash, you ain't getting a band).

2. The style and format of your wedding (a harp is no-go at a biker wedding).

3. Your taste (no-one wants to hear the 'Sesame Street' theme at your wedding, no matter how cute you think it is).

4. How insistent your parents are that you have a waltz ('But darling, it's traditional...').

Let's look at the various aspects of the day.

Before the service
It is likely that your first guests will turn up half an hour early. When you add on 15 minutes for bride lateness, that's a long time to be amused by reading through the Order of Service looking for spelling mistakes.

Appropriate music will set the tone for the wedding and get your guests in a festive and celebratory mood.

Traditional church style weddings tend towards live music, particularly of the 'big-organ' variety.

Most churches will have a recommended organist and a list of standards, which they can crank out ad infinitum. The organ provides a certain air of tradition and formality. If you want to do something different, a harp or string quartet will do the trick. Sure, they're expensive, but there's nothing quite like it when those strings kick off with the opening of Pachelbel's Canon.

For an outdoor or garden wedding, a decent CD player should meet your needs.

CDs have several advantages: they don't cost much, you have total control over the selection, you know exactly what you're getting, you can stick them on 'repeat' to cope with extended bridal lateness, they don't make mistakes, the sound quality is good, and you can have some of the world's greatest musos playing at your wedding rather than some three-chord wonder.

The music should reflect the style of your wedding while at the same time promoting a sense of occasion. There's nothing to stop you having jazz, contemporary, acoustic or anything by Frank Sinatra. Classical music always goes down a treat, as long as its nothing by Schoenberg, whose music is the tonal equivalent of a train crashing into a truck carrying dynamite which is parked outside a cutlery factory.

Don't be tempted to 'be original' and play a TV tunes CD.

And if the guy who takes the bookings at the function centre says he has a brother called Enzo who can play his accordion at your wedding for next to nothing, politely decline the offer.

Just trust me.

The arrival of the bride

One of the most stereotypical aspects of your wedding day is that single millisecond when all your months of planning and expectation come crashing in to one single indefinable *I'll-remember-this-on-my-death-bed* moment, and your guests all suck in air and get to their feet, and turn, and a general hush falls over the assembly and the sun filters through the stained glass of the apostle Paul (if in a church) or through the canopy of verdant foliage above (if in a garden).

This is what you've been waiting for.

There she is, your almost-wife, resplendent and stunning. The rest of the world fades into darkness and there's only her moving towards you as if in a tunnel of light. The processional begins... with the staccato theme from *Psycho*.

Eeeggch! Eeeggch! Eeeggch! Eeeggch! Eeeggch!

No, wait a minute!

That's not right!

Appropriate music is in order. If your bride is going to make a grand entrance (as opposed to the two of you walking in together, or something radical like that), then you should have music which is celebratory.

If your name is Hamish Donalbain McDonald and you're marrying Eileen McAngus-McBanquo, for example, it is likely that a bagpipe fanfare will be on the cards.

Or if you're having a Star Trek theme wedding... well, you know the rest.

You can always go the traditional 'Here comes the bride, all fat and wide', which is actually Wagner's 'Wedding March' from *Lohengrin*. It's clichéd, but sounds great if played well on a decent organ or if you have a good orchestral CD version and a monster PA. My other favourite is Purcell's Trumpet Voluntary.

Of course, there's nothing stopping you playing some suitable contemporary music. I would suggest however, that you avoid the following titles:

- 'The Song of the Volga Boatmen'
- 'The Bitch is Back'
- 'I've Loved Many a Woman and You were Almost the Best
- 'Howzat (You messed about, I caught you out)'
- 'Get your Biscuits in the Oven and your Buns in Bed'
- 'Highway to Hell'
- 'The Chicken Dance'

During the wedding

Church weddings lend themselves to the singing of hymns.

I have been to some weddings where the hymnal singing has been so stirring it has made my skin prickle. You know, strong melodies, terrific harmonies, moving words and a woman up the back somewhere cranking out a blood-boiling descant. (In this regard, I can thoroughly recommend 'Oh for a Thousand Tongues', 'And Can it Be', 'For All the Saints', 'Amazing Grace' or 'I Wanna Rock'n'Roll All Nite').

But be warned.

I have also been to weddings where they thought they'd *do the traditional thang* and have hymns, but they failed to register the fact that none of their friends or rellies knew any of the tunes, which really didn't matter because none of them could sing anyway, and the cumulative result was something akin to an asthmatic cat drowning inside a bagpipe, and the only thing my skin was doing was trying to crawl off and slither out the back door.

So if you're going to have communal singing, weigh up whether or not it's going to be a stirring triumph or a musical nightmare.

If you're getting married in a garden or hall or other non-church venue, hymns probably won't even come into the equation. But a lot of couples still like the idea of a mid-ceremony musical interlude anyway. This could be an item on its own, or an accompaniment to the signing of the register.

If you have muso mates, get a duet or a little band or choir going. Just make sure they're good. And don't let them get carried away. I went to a wedding where, during the signing of the register, the bride's brother got up and sang. Then the sister and some of her friends got up and did a flute ensemble thing. Then a group of friends got up and did a few choral numbers. Only to be followed by the big acoustic guitar jam session by several persons unknown to me. Which preceded the father of the groom singing some old song that contained the words 'romp-de-bomp' in one of the verses.

It was like a freakin' talent quest!

Some people started walking out. Including me.

Your guests are there to see you get married. If they want a show, they'll go to *The Sound of Music*.

Recessional

The recessional is the piece of music played at the end of the wedding after you've said what you have to say and signed what you have to sign and then the minister or celebrant or jumqua or whoever turns to everybody and says, that's all folks.

There's usually a general noise of approval from the gathered throng, falling anywhere on the scale from happy sighs to riotous hoots of delight.

At this point you can stampede out like you're running down the streets of Pamplona. This is what they do in the movies, usually under a hail of rice or confetti. (However, most churches and registries won't let you do it, because it's such a dog to clean up. Which reminds me of when my cousin got married, and one of her friends threw rice on the couple as they came out of the church, but the problem was that the rice had been cooked...)

If you are going to do the barnstorm-the-back-door thing, then you need some anthemic music of triumph. Some favourites are:

- Wagner's Overture to 'The Mastersingers of Nuremberg'
- Beethoven's Symphony No. 9 in D Minor, Opus 125 (fourth movement)

- John Williamson's *Star Wars* (Jedi Theme)
- Vivaldi's The Four Seasons, Opus 8 No. 1 ('Spring') or No.2 ('Harvest')
- Mendelssohn's Wedding March (from *A Midsummer Night's Dream*)
- Handel's Hallelujah chorus
- The Knack's 'My Sharona'
- Frank Sinatra's 'I Get a Kick out of You', 'Love and Marriage' or 'I've Got You Under My Skin'
- Ella Fitzgerald and Louis Armstrong's 'They Can't Take That Away from Me'

Given that your bride probably picked the processional music, use your newly acquired marital negotiation skills and claim the recessional as your own. Remember, it's *your* wedding too.

If she doesn't come to the party, threaten to withhold your sexual favours for the first month of marriage.

No, wait.

Bad idea.

Reception

Right. The wedding service is over and you're married. Great. Now the party can begin.

I have seen pianists and string quartets at formal receptions, jazz trios at trendy receptions and bush bands in backyards. I have listened to nice CDs in restaurants and family homes, and put up with a hideous rock band in a hall. I have even been tortured by a maître d' who took it upon himself to sing the theme from 'The Love Boat' in a thick Italian accent. He used a radio mike and worked the room like a bad nightclub singer. It was a new insight into the words 'truly appalling'.

If you're doing the music'n'dancing thing, you can hire a mobile DJ who'll do all the sound, lights and music and maybe even a mirrorball and smoke machine if you want to get silly. They're usually well experienced in wedding protocol and have a travelling library of suitable material. But it is imperative that you ask to see their playlist. Musical tastes vary and you don't want to find out on the night that your DJ has the world's biggest collection of international line-dancing hits.

Make clear exactly what you want at the various stages of the function. You might, for example, have a preference for intimate slow dancing, or big speed-metal stage-diving, or mindless thumping dance-party mega-mix.

I would also suggest you tell the DJ that at the end of the night you don't want the hokey-pokey or 'For They are Jolly Good Fellows' or the macarena.

Watch the birdie

Everyone say, 'hol-i-days'.

TODD, WEDDING PHOTOGRAPHER

A friend of mine got married in an old stone church.

As we piled through the door at the conclusion of the service, suddenly the crowd stopped and backed up into the church. There was mass confusion and I had the momentary sensation of being in an English soccer riot.

It turned out that the videographer had not been quick enough moving his equipment from Point A to Point B and, as a consequence, had missed the critical confetti moment of bride and groom emerging from the church.

So, we had to do a replay.

As we were backing up, the videographer got up on a chair and gave directions. The lucky couple were to push the doors open and stand together on the church steps, while the guests, like a flowing river of love (his words), were to pour out of the church in two rivulets around them. Meanwhile, he would pan back and dissolve out. His final words were, 'And don't forget to look happy, happy, happy!'

Practicalities

As far as I was concerned, this was taking the idea of 'capturing valuable memories' to a ridiculous extreme.

Don't get me wrong, it's nice to have memories of the day, and photographers and videographers do provide a valuable service at most weddings. Years from now you'll giggle at the photos showing your out-of-date haircut, unfashionable glasses and ridiculously antiquated bow tie. Your children will be fascinated by how youthful and vibrant you looked on videotape (before they came along and ruined your lives).

But it is not universally ordained that your wedding will be photographed and videoed. I was best man at a wedding where the happy couple banned photos and videos because they considered them an unnecessary distraction. They wanted to concentrate on each other without having to 'say cheese'.

If you are going to have cameras at your wedding, think carefully about their use.

Once upon a time, a photographer just wandered around and snapped off a few rolls. Sure, they might have shoved a few rellies together for a couple of staged shots, but that was it.

Nowadays, couples are increasingly going for 'a shoot' in between the service and reception. No longer satisfied with formal shots of guests arranged in order of height in front of a giant fireplace, they go out on location to try to emulate the arty shots they've been drooling over for months in magazines. This is all well and good for them, but it's a bit of a drag for the guests who are stuck with three hours to kill and a babysitter charging by the hour. On behalf of your guests, can I humbly request that we put an end to this annoying and self-indulgent practice. This is the one day of your life when all your friends and family will be gathered together. Don't abandon them!

As with most aspects of your wedding, it's up to the two of you how photos and/or video will play a part in your day.

You could be low-key about the whole thing. Have a competent photographic mate do the work, ask your friends to post you copies of their photos, or give a video camera to your cousin. On the up side, it only costs you the price of film and a few bottles of wine as presents. On the down side, you end up with red-eye photos and distant trees sprouting out of people's heads, and a video that zooms in and out like it's on a bungee cord.

A popular trend at the moment is to put disposable cameras on each table at the reception. On the good side, you are guaranteed of a wide range of casual amateur shots. On the bad side, you are also guaranteed of a set of under-the-table 'upskirt' shots and, if you're really lucky, maybe even a few snapped off in a toilet cubicle.

Alternatively, there's the professional option.

Professional photography costs a lot, but then again, you only get married once (in theory). And at the end of the day, all you have left are your memories, some photos and ten cheese platters.

Professionals have more experience in shooting weddings and, if they're good, they'll manage to get quality material while being unobtrusive. They work efficiently and provide direction when needed. They have better equipment for post-production and arty shots, and you'll get a polished finished product.

Like artists, photographers have their own distinctive styles, so shop around to find someone who suits your taste.

Word of mouth is a reliable starting point. Look at the photos/video of friends who have been recently married and ask for recommendations. Check out the bridal supplements or classifieds in your local paper for photos of newlyweds. Contact a couple of different businesses and look at their brochures, pamphlets or sample albums or videos.

You will cross some off your list straight away (bridal party standing in a line with arms by their sides and the tallest guy with no forehead). Others will have a particular look or style that appeals to you (photojournalist b & w snap of bridal party laughing and walking along beach with shoes off).

When you've found someone whose work you like, it's time to talk specifics and negotiate. Go through the details with a fine-tooth comb, otherwise you might end up with a nasty surprise. Read the fine print. You might ask them, for example: How much for additional hours of coverage, reprints or extra copies of the video? Is there an extra charge for special effects or location shots? Are the negatives included? If not, how much are they? Have they ever taken paparazzi shots of someone famous in the nude, and if so, can you get copies? Is there a written contract or guarantee that stipulates the conditions?

Once you've decided on a company, ask to meet the actual person who'll be turning up on your wedding day. Their friendliness factor may be important to you. I was best man at a wedding where the photographer was this grimy, grumpy guy who spent the day scratching his butt and looking bored out of his brain. His photos were great, but he was not pleasant to be near. (I found out later he was a police photographer, whose full-time job was to photograph dead people at crime scenes. We should have realised when he tried to draw a chalk outline around the bride and groom.)

You might also want to let any camera-folk know if you're having a la-de-da formal wedding so that they can dress appropriately. If you have a room full of penguin suits and pearls, you don't want someone walking around wearing baggy jeans and old sandshoes. (Though if they are a professional, they should dress like one ... particularly with the money they're charging you.)

Run through the program of the day with the person standing on the other side of the lens and tell them what shots you want. It may even be worthwhile producing a list of group shots so that in the hecticness of the day you don't forget anyone. It would be a pity if you forgot to have your photo taken with Nanna, who flew all the way from Greece, now wouldn't it?

Oh...one more thing before you slap down the plastic.

If you get married by a celebrant or at a registry office, it's likely that there will be minimal restrictions on the use of cameras, tripods and flashes.

Churches, however, can be a different matter.

Many ministers have specific rules about the use of photographic equipment during the service. At our wedding, for example, the minister made it quite clear that he wanted the focus to be on us and our vows. He did not want the distractions of video crews, flashes and motor-driven cameras whining away.

But he was happy for a set video to film the service and for photos to be taken before and after the vows. At one point he even invited people to come up for close-ups.

I was at one wedding where a video operator almost climbed in between the bride and groom to get an up-close action shot right in the middle of their vows. It was very annoying, and the minister quite rightly told him to shog off.

So run through the service with the person officiating and communicate 'the deal' clearly to the people holding the cameras.

Whether a friend snaps off a few rolls or you have Steven Spielberg behind the camera, your happy memories will be captured forever. You'll come back from your honeymoon and show your photo albums and three-hour video to anyone who visits you for the next six months.

Then you'll put the whole lot in a shoebox at the back of the linen cupboard and get them out only every decade or so.

'I do': the most important bit

With this ring, I wed you.

PRAYER BOOK

A mate of mine, who is a Christian minister, had a meeting with a young couple who wanted to get married in his church.

They arrived at the rectory and, after introductions, started talking about their relationship and the seriousness of marital commitment. But my friend was soon cut off by the rather impatient groom who asked if, before they went much further, they could check out the church building.

So over they went.

The groom immediately began clambering all over the building, looking at lighting possibilities and backgrounds and inspecting the carpet and sandstone and snapping off photos of the church decor, stained glass and portico. He even had a fiddle on the old organ.

The bride, meanwhile, was pacing out the steps down the aisle, while humming some vacuous Celine Dion tune. She repeated this process five or six times.

My mate humoured them for a while but eventually got fed up and started to talk about the vows they would be saying.

'Look,' called the bride in mid-step halfway down the aisle, 'We'll just [*step-pause-pause*] say the standard thing. You just tell us what to say [*step-pause-pause*] on the day.'

'Yeah, whatever,' yelled the groom while lining up a shot of the registry table. 'We're not fussed.'

'Actually,' said my mate with the ever-so-subtle tone of impatience in his voice, 'The vows are the most important part of the day. I think we should run through them beforehand.'

The bride broke from the theme from *Titanic* to respond with, 'No, the most important part of the day [*step-pause-pause*] is me not stuffing up my walk down the aisle.'

My mate smiled and then told them to get out of his church and stop wasting his time.

The attitude of this couple is not uncommon. When it comes to planning the actual wedding service, it's easy to get hung-up on the peripherals — the hire cars, red carpet, lighting, flowers, candelabras, marquees, waiters, seating arrangements, poems, romantic music, orders-of-service and the positioning of photographers, videographers and the string quartet.

Don't get me wrong. Good organisation is part and parcel of a smoothly run wedding service. However, all the froth and bubble should not eclipse the real purpose of the event.

The legal necessities

A wedding is a public ceremony where all your friends, relatives and acquaintances witness you declare your commitment to another person and, even if you're already living together, *officially* and formally launch a new phase of your life. And in doing so, whether you're getting married in a church, office, mountaintop restaurant, lounge room or shark-filled tank, the most important part is the ceremony itself.

If you were to cut the ceremony of marriage right back to its bare bones, if you were to put it into a mortar and pestle it down into a singular, primary element, it would be this: *a promise*.

In fact, the word 'wedding' (from the Anglo-Saxon word 'wed') means *pledge*. It is a vow, a cross-my-heart-and-hope-to-die (with no fingers crossed behind your back) covenant between you and a woman to form a new family unit and be committed to each other and love each other and nurse and serve and nurture and encourage and support and have (exclusive) sex with each other for ever and ever, amen.

Such a significant and life-changing pledging is not done lightly. (Fortunately for you, unlike the guys in the Old Testament, who held each other's scrotums when they made a covenant, modern ceremonies are a little more dignified. Maybe that's because your fiancée doesn't have a scrotum. At least, you *hope* she doesn't have a scrotum. You'll soon find out if she *does* have a scrotum...)

To be legal, your marriage must be officiated by a person approved by the government, and while the words and rituals vary from place to place, the pledging basically involves the public and formal declaration of two things:

1. There's no reason why I shouldn't be married.
2. I want you [insert name here] to be my wife...if that's okay with you. (The old medieval vow made by the wife — 'I promise to be debonair and buxom, in bed and at board' — is sadly no longer required.)

To make it official, you sign a certificate...and that's it.

It's simpler than joining a video club. You're married.

The no-frills service

The closest thing to the 'no-frills' ceremony is the registry wedding, which is conducted in a nicely decorated room in a government building. Generally, you have the choice of business hours Monday to Saturday and perhaps also one evening in the week. Beware of Saturdays: they're the sausage-grinder day on which a busy registry office might churn through 14 weddings between nine and five.

There is no dress code, although you are encouraged to wear clothing suitable for the import of the occasion. Most couples wear nice clothes (suit and tie for men, formal dress for women), with morning suits and wedding gowns only making very rare appearances. At the other end of the scale, others do the jeans and T-shirt thing.

... the jeans and T-shirt thing

A registry wedding takes about half an hour, is inexpensive and doesn't require endless nights of planning or production. And while the words 'registry office' don't inspire romantic confidence, you will find that the room is a nice, formal area, appropriately elegant for such a serious ceremony. (It's not an office with computers and phones ringing and a secretary chewing gum and doing her nails, saying, 'What'd ya say yer name was again?')

The service itself is brief and to the point, lacking in religious reference. There are no crucifixes or stained-glass windows of Jesus staring down at you, and there is only minimal room for 'personal touches' — like a song for the introduction, or the wearing of animal outfits, togas or pirate suits.

I read an interview recently with ten couples who got married in a registry office. Their reasons for choosing a registry wedding over a church service or an elaborate private wedding were many and varied, and included: because the bride was pregnant and a church wedding seemed inappropriate; because it was a second marriage for both and they'd already done the garden wedding once before; because they wanted a quick and no-fuss wedding; because they couldn't afford a big production; because the groom wanted to wear a black T-shirt, joggers and boardshorts; because they hated the pretentiousness of a big service and formal clothing; because all their friends and family were overseas; because they wanted to surprise everybody by announcing it at their 'engagement party' that very night (what I wouldn't give to be a fly on the wall!).

The registry wedding is very appealing to some couples, particularly those whose best friends have just got married and they have witnessed all the trauma and headaches first-hand.

The extra-frills service

Some couples, however, desire more of an event. This is their one wedding day, and they want it to be 'extra-ordinary', memorable, special, and conducted with a splash of fanfare. Instead of the in-and-out 'microwave dinner' version, they want the silver service extravaganza.

Such a service, regardless of venue, still has the legal pledges, but over the years has developed a number of rituals, which make it longer and more elaborate.

The rituals vary around the world.

For example, an ancient Finn bride and groom ritually swallowed a flaming piece of fungus; during a Shinto ceremony, the couple drink rice wine together; Kumi couples cuddle a mongo tree to sanctify their marriage; traditional Papuans sit back to back in the middle of a circle of guests who then spit water over them; staunch Steuerite couples have their hands tied to each other's by ribbons; Jews smash an empty wine glass underfoot; a Locola bride chews up a pithy red berry and spits it in her husband's mouth; and I won't mention what Vikings did with selected body parts of their conquered enemies to liven up *their* wedding services.

Western wedding services are rife with equally quirky traditions. The modern wedding ceremony has picked up a number of rituals over the years and is now a bizarre amalgam of traditional baggage, romantic ideals and religious custom: the groom 'waiting' at the church; the bride's mother in a big hat; the role of ushers and bridesmaids and matrons of honour and best men and groomsmen; the grand (late) arrival in vintage cars; the bride wearing a once-only white extravaganza; the something-old-new-borrowed-blue thing; the processional; the bride being 'given away'; the exchanging (and wearing) of wedding rings; the 'kissing of the bride'; the groom fainting at the altar; communion (eating bread and drinking wine); musicians playing 12-string guitars; the recessional; the throwing of confetti...Such rituals are now almost indistinguishable from the legal necessities.

To people who spit berries, swallow fungus and make hand puppets out of scrotums, Western wedding customs are just as weird as their customs are to us.

Which leads us to your two most pressing questions. If you are to go beyond the registry wedding and have a more elaborate service, you will be asking:

1. *Where are you going to get married?*
2. *Who is going to 'do the marrying'?*

The answers to these questions will very much dictate the style, feel and content of your wedding service. Your job, in these planning days, is to work out with your bride (and the other key players) what sort of wedding service you are going to have. It will reflect your personalities, tastes, dreams, philosophies about life, religious backgrounds, family traditions, finances and how domineering your mothers are.

The religious service

Traditionally, wedding services have taken place in a church or temple. In fact, the mere mention of the word 'wedding' conjures up a mental picture of a bride walking down a carpeted aisle, organ blasting away, sun filtering through stained-glass windows, and the robed minister beginning with the words, 'Dearly beloved, we are gathered here today...'

You may want a religious ceremony for a number of reasons: because of your beliefs, because it's 'the done thing', because of the aforementioned romantic imagery, because all your family have been married in the same church, because that's what you've always imagined, or maybe it's just the nice architecture for your wedding photos...

Practicalities

If you are not a member of a church, finding the right one, like everything else, is a matter of shopping around. The photogenic quality of the church may be of prime importance in your mind, but I would encourage you to seriously examine *the service itself* to see if it's appropriate for you.

Some ministers may allow you flexibility in modifying or omitting parts of the service. At the opposite end of the spectrum, other ministers will permit no budging, and you may even be required to start attending the church or do a short marriage course. If you don't like it, bad luck.

A church wedding service is 'set' according to the doctrines and traditions of the religion or denomination, although there may be a few different services from which to choose. The 'pledging' process is more detailed and elaborate. There are, for example, the well known phrases — 'Till death do us part', 'Promise to love, honour and serve', 'For better, for worse, for richer, for poorer', '[Name], will you take [Name] as your wife?' 'With this ring I wed you', 'Do you want fries with that?' — as well as a selection of hymns or songs, prayers for marriage and children, Bible readings, candle lighting, a short address, bungee jumping and maybe even communion. Consider very carefully if this kind of wedding service is relevant to you.

You see, the very point of a church wedding is that you are making your promises 'in the sight of God' because 'marriage is a gift from God' and 'marriage is the symbol of God's undying love' and 'marriage is in accordance with God's purpose' and 'those who marry otherwise than God's word are not joined together by God'. Do you notice the recurring theme here? Even the grand announcement, the climax of the whole thing, is when the minister says, 'In the name of God, I declare them to be husband and wife.'

The point is that God features heavily in a church wedding service. Which is understandable when you think about it. After all, it's His place.

This is great if you are a God-fearing person, but if you're not, carefully read through the service — especially the vows — and ask yourself if it has any meaning for you.

If you don't believe in God, there's not much point centring your promises around Him. Nor is there much sense in singing hymns of praise and praying if you don't believe He's listening. Nor is it meaningful having readings from the Bible if you think it's just some old book.

Perhaps for these reasons, religious weddings now account for less than half of all weddings, with civil ceremonies (a registry wedding or a celebrant wedding) now taking over as the most popular form of wedding service.

The DIY service

A civil ceremony conducted by a registered celebrant is the do-it-yourself wedding option. For it to be legal, you still have to say the required important bits, but after that, it's a bit of a free-for-all. There is a lot more flexibility in the service itself, and as such, you have an opportunity to create a service that has a high level of meaning for both of you.

A celebrant will often give you a rough plan or a few ideas, but the rest is up to you. Many people throw in a favourite tune, some poetry or some inspirational writings. I know of one musical couple who sang a love song from an opera to each other as part of their vows. Another couple had their guests come forward and each light a candle of love, the flame of which would illuminate and bless their relationship and the smoke of which would rise up as a symbol of their something-or-other new-age mystical spiritual whatsit. Another couple went for a swim in the middle of their service to represent the cleansing of their bodies in preparation for their lives ahead. Basically you can do whatever you want to make your wedding memorable and meaningful.

You may prefer a celebrant service for any number of reasons: perhaps a religious ceremony has no meaning for you; perhaps you want more input and want to write your own vows; or perhaps you have a penchant for a particular location or venue ...like the ten-pin bowling alley where you first met.

You may find a celebrant wedding particularly appealing if you both come from different religious traditions and no single church can accommodate you. If your bride is a voodoo priestess, for example, and you can't find a church willing to accommodate the sacrifice of a live goat on the altar, a celebrant might be the answer for you. I went to one wedding where the Catholic bride couldn't get married in her Catholic church because her groom was Protestant, but the Catholic family refused to have the wedding in a Protestant church. As a consequence, they had a celebrant do a messy amalgam of a wedding service that drew on both traditions.

Finding the right celebrant is a matter of looking in the phone book or local paper or on the internet (or, preferably, getting a recommendation from a friend) and having a chat with the celebrant about what they do and what they offer and what they charge. They'll often have their own reading material, and even supply their own bits and pieces like a table, cloth, candles, chairs and ribbons.

Celebrant weddings are very flexible because you can have them wherever you want — on a beach, in a tennis court, at the ninth hole, on a boat, in the lounge room or in a car park — although they'll charge you through the teeth if you want to do any wacky stuff like get married on the wing of a biplane.

But to get back to an earlier point, while an interesting, personal and well-planned wedding is desirable, in the grand scheme of things it ultimately doesn't matter where you get married or whether you and your bride turn up separately or together or what you're wearing or whether your guests sit in a circle or rows or how many songs you have or how many doves you release... the important bit is the promises you make.

Choose and say your words carefully. They should reflect the depth of your respect and love and your desire for a lifelong commitment to each other.

If you are writing your own vows, good words and phrases to include are: 'respect', 'love', 'cherish', 'serve', 'honour', 'for the rest of our lives', 'listen', 'breakfast in bed', 'be there for you', 'desire', 'forever', 'I promise not to have sex with anyone else, even if there's no way you could possibly ever find out about it'.

Words and phrases to be avoided in your wedding vows are: 'affair', 'pumpkins', 'as long as I feel like it', 'sex on demand', 'until you become ugly', 'servant', 'peasant', 'beggar', 'leper', 'orgy', 'barefoot, pregnant and in the kitchen', 'toilet-cleaning duties', 'jugs', 'do as I tell you and don't argue with me, woman'.

By the way, at the conclusion of the service you may be tempted to adopt an old English custom whereby the wedding guests litter the aisle with objects representative of the husband's trade. The newlyweds then walk over these as they leave the church. So, for example, a carpenter and his bride would find their wedding path strewn with wood shavings.

This is fine if you are a florist or silk importer.

Go for it.

However, if you are a proctologist or circumcision surgeon, or if you work on a production line making urinal fragrance tablets, I suggest you forget this quaint custom.

5
Let's Celebrate
(letting your hair down)

'We did all the expected things, like the bridal waltz. But the most memorable were the ones from us, not from the book. Slam dancing to Nirvana and getting rumbled in the farewell circle ... now that's what a good reception should be ... a good party. You remember the things that make your wedding different from anyone else's.'

AARON

Reception basics

I hate receptions. Receptions are a nightmare.
ANONYMOUS VENUE MANAGER

Your marriage service (i.e. the part where you say 'I do') is an important ritual that signifies a new and exciting stage in your life. It is only fitting that such a momentous event is witnessed by those close to you. They will come from far and wide to watch the spectacle. Some will come because they want to see you pledge your love to another and take your rightful place in the circle of life. Others will come because there'll be a good feed afterwards, and all it will cost them is the price of the cheap breadknife they will get you as a present.

In fact, your wedding is one of the few times when pretty well everyone you know from the various and separate parts of your life (as well as those distant rellies from interstate whom you've never met) will travel great distances, get all dressed up in nice clothes, and be in the one place at the one time with you as the co-centre of attention. (The other event will be your funeral, but let's not go into that now.)

As it's a festive event attended by all the 'special' people in your life, it is only fitting that after the official hoo-ha is over and you are relishing your first moments as newlyweds you celebrate, carouse, whoop it up, kick up your heels and party on. The technical term for this shebang is a 'reception'.

In some cultures, the marriage celebration (reception) is an all-night hypnotic frenzy of dancing around a blazing inferno followed by the mass slaughter and wholesale consumption of a variety of defenceless animals. Most receptions I go to, though, tend to be a little more sedate. You know, nice suits and hairdos, setting sun, speech with a few gags, fumbled waltz to the theme from *Dirty Dancing* followed by the bride's Uncle Malcolm falling over at the bar.

The party

Your job is to work out what sort of party or reception you will have to celebrate your marriage. My guess is that you'll want more than just a few balloons on the pavement outside the registry, but you probably won't want to go as far as the reception held in 1981 for Mohammed Al Maktoum and his bride Princess Salama, which lasted seven days and cost about $50 million.

Two factors will influence your choice of reception:

1. Economics

Let's get this straight right now. Wedding receptions can be hideously expensive. Even a small affair at a local restaurant will put a considerable ding in your wallet. It's even worse once you get into the league of long guest lists, set menus, drinks packages and decoration options ('What better way to make your special day even more special than by illuminating the room into a fairyland of love with candles and a sprig of ivy on every table? Lacy tablecloths at a nominal extra fee...').

Even if you *can* afford to pay an enormous sum for a reception, that doesn't necessarily mean it's a good idea to do so. You might decide that nothing that lasts six hours can be worth a year's wages. Some friends of mine decided on a low-key reception when they got married, and with the rest of the money they saved bought furniture and extended their honeymoon by four days.

It amazes me that some people spend their lives working and saving and scrimping and managing their money well (they're the sort of people who'll spend an entire day wandering around shops searching for the best price on a toaster), but at the mention of the word 'wedding' their brain switches off and all of a sudden it makes perfectly good economic sense to spend the equivalent of a deposit on a house on a single dinner for 50 people.

In conclusion, ask yourself the question: how much is a reasonable amount to spend?

2. *Style*

Your wedding reception is a party, and that party should reflect your personalities and needs — whether it's a picnic with cut sandwiches on paper plates by the sea, or a formal extravaganza with truffles wrapped in bacon on silver platters in a ballroom.

When Meredith and I got married, our main desire was to celebrate with *all* our friends and relatives. We wanted everyone we knew to be there on our special day.

Sure, the idea of an extravagant and expensive reception was appealing (in a bridal-magazine kind of way), but not so appealing as to make us halve our guest list.

So we had an enormous afternoon tea in the church hall instead, to which everyone was welcome. We decorated the hall ourselves and played our own selection of music. Caterers did all the finger food (of which there was plenty), friends did the flower arrangements and we hired nice tablecloths and boxes of crockery and glassware from a local company.

It was a great success: classy, subtle, not too costly and very, very festive. Everyone had a great time in the noisy confusion, especially Meredith and me.

Best of all, heaps of people came and we were absolutely thrilled with their presents... um, I mean their *presence*.

Being creative

When planning your wedding reception, assume nothing. Remember what I've said before? Start with a blank slate, not a blueprint of every other wedding you've been to. For example, you could have:

- no reception at all (there's a new one!)
- dinner with just the bridal party
- a small reception for immediate family and friends in a restaurant
- a barbecue or spit by the river
- a formal bash in your backyard with waiters and a guy in a white hat who carves the meat
- a lunch followed by an informative tour of the local abattoir
- a buffet with dancing in a private room of a club
- a picnic in a park, banquet on a beach, festivities in a field, hoedown in a hall, fun on a ferry or soiree in the sun at the South Pole in summer
- a cocktail party at a lookout
- bangers and mash at a pub
- a moving reception in a 'cruising' double-decker bus or on a river or harbour ferry
- a breakfast, morning or afternoon tea

I have been to some fantastic weddings over the years, from the most exclusive and expensive black-tie affair to an absolute humdinger with a bush band in someone's backyard.

It's your wedding day, and you should have a party that you and your guests will enjoy and remember, no matter how big or small it is.

Details, details

If you're catering in your backyard, make sure you cover all the basics — tables, chairs, marquee, lighting, sound system, waiters, chefs, linen, cutlery, crockery, serving area. You can either hire these yourself or have a catering firm do the whole lot, which certainly would save you a lot of fuss.

If you are having a reception in a restaurant, club, hotel or function centre, you will need to shop around. Most venues will have an information pack containing all the menus and prices and drinks packages and miscellaneous options.

Be careful with the drinks packages: the prices of most of these seem based on the assumption that every guest will drink an entire case of beer and several bottles of good wine. You may be better off ditching the package and paying for just what is consumed, but make sure you check out the standard bar price list first, and make clear what is to be excluded from the tab. All it takes is a few mates knocking down double bourbons, imported lagers and vintage reds and you'll be filing for bankruptcy. Also, it's a good idea to check out if there are extra labour costs associated with drinks on the lawn or on the upper verandah or whatever.

Be careful with the food, too. Know exactly what you are getting. Catering firms and function centres have an annoying habit of giving their ordinary food extraordinary names, which also allows them to charge extraordinary prices. A 'skewered beef sirloin drizzled with bush tomatoes' may sound good, but you'll be annoyed when it turns out to be a cocktail frankfurter on a toothpick with tomato sauce. I looked at a couple of wedding menus and was stumped by items like vegetable nori, mini mille-feuilles, prawn blinis, kipfler potatoes, pesto croutes, spinach roulade, wind-dried salmon, polenta cups, filo kisses with akudjura, gnocchi with pecorino, toasted brioche, paupiettes of perch, a macedoine of vegetables, tomato concasse and a partridge in a pear tree.

Function venues usually have a coordinator who will discuss your plans and make suggestions. They also coordinate the show and make sure that everything runs like clockwork on the day, leaving you to relax.

No matter what sort of reception you have, or how big or small it is, plan it well. Finalise all the details in advance and make sure everyone knows what their various jobs are. On the day itself, you don't want to be running around paying cheques, organising transport or carrying presents out to your car. Have it all set so that you can hang loose and enjoy the company of your wife and your guests.

Then again, it doesn't matter how much you organise it, there'll always be some prat who, just as the food is being served and you're sitting with your new bride enjoying her delicious company, tells you that they are vegetarian, allergic to seafood, on a carbohydrate-free diet and that dairy foods give them diarrhoea.

Just nod, smile and tell them to shog off.

Reception traditions

When Phil told me it was normal in his family for the bride and groom to rub cake in each other's faces, I thought he was kidding.

SIOBHAN

A wedding reception contains a panoply of unique and unusual traditions, customs and rituals. And I suspect that most couples automatically incorporate these into their day without so much as a moment's thought or discussion.

Some of these rituals are fun; some serve a purpose; others are pointless and embarrassing. They are not written in law and, surprisingly, your marriage will not be annulled if you don't subscribe to them.

Here's a quick run-through of some of the standard fare. When it comes time to decide what is going to happen at your reception, take or leave these traditions as you see fit.

The bridal car

Standard wedding transport for the bridal party on the day is often in a hired limo, vintage car or classic vehicle. It's probably one of the few times in your life you'll have a chauffeur and a ride in a prestige car, and for many couples, the idea of cruising along in their wedding clothes sipping champagne is a long-standing middle-class wedding fantasy. You get to feel important in the traffic, where people wave at you and honk their horns, and the occasional bozo yells out, 'Don't do it! Don't do it!' And besides, it's the ultimate wedding photo cliché.

A prestige wedding car adds to the specialness of the day. Some couples even go for something more creative, like a London cab, a vintage bus, a Harley Davidson with sidecar, a horse and buggy or a fleet of minis.

Many couples get friends or relatives with nice cars to do the job. All you need is a bit of ribbon to make their V8 look the part, and faith in the fact that the owners will clean out all the hamburger wrappers from the back seat.

Then again, there's nothing to stop you driving yourself in your own car.

The best wedding fleet I've witnessed consisted of four convertible bright-red classic 50s' Fords. It looked fantastic, the bridal party heading off with their tops down (the cars, not the bridesmaids) in the summer sun, all dressed up and drinking champagne. Unfortunately, the wind factor destroyed about $300 worth of hairdos in less than four minutes.

The receiving line
This is the official welcoming party that 'receives' the guests as they arrive at the reception.

According to tradition, the receiving line is typically made up of the bride's mother and father, the groom's mother and father, the bride and groom followed by the chief attendants — although in reality it can be whoever you want. At really large formal functions, an announcer presents the guests to the receiving line, but this is a bit over-the-top at a small function.

The receiving line is the only structured event during the entire wedding day when the guests get to formally greet the bride and groom and, where appropriate, meet the parents. It also allows whoever is footing the bill to look into the eyes of the people who are costing them a fortune.

The disadvantage of the receiving line is that you get stuck by the front door for an hour instead of getting on with the good stuff inside with all your friends.

The other disadvantage is that some of your no-brains guests will bring their presents to the reception (the ultimate faux pas in wedding etiquette) and want to hand them to you as you stand there, which according to all the books is tacky, tacky, tacky. Best to have a table *before* the receiving line so they can dump their toasters there.

We didn't have a receiving line at our reception, because we had 250 guests and it would have taken six hours to get through them, to say nothing of the whole passing-germs-along-the-line thing.

The archway of love
I went to a wedding once where, after a lengthy session of champagne and aperitifs on the lawn, we were invited (finally) to enter the dining room. In the middle of the door was an archway of roses, and we all had to squeeze through it while a short Italian man in an old suit sang a song about the fragrance of roses rising to heaven and blessing the love of the happy couple, and other vomit like that.

I've encountered this at no other wedding, so you may be spared.

MC
MC stands for Master of Ceremonies — or, in this politically correct age, Person of Ceremonies (although I much prefer the more salacious connotations that 'Mistress of Ceremonies' conjures up; many wedding receptions are boring affairs and I think a woman straight out of one of those late-night adult phone services, with high heels and a whip, would liven things up considerably...).

The MC is like the ringmaster at a circus. He or she makes the introductions and announcements, tells the people what's going on and keeps the whole event running smoothly...although hopefully your MC won't wear a candy-striped vest and carry a whip.

Handing over to the MC the responsibility of the running of

the formalities at your reception allows you to sit back and enjoy yourself. That way, you don't have to be checking with the kitchen staff about courses, or chasing your guests to sit down so things can get started.

In choosing an MC, you want someone who is confident, organised, on time, trustworthy, independent and able to solve problems. A splash of personality, creativity and humour wouldn't go astray either.

Also, be aware that if you choose someone who has been on a wild boys' weekend away with you, you can bet they'll mention the time you went for a midnight nudie-run wearing a gorilla mask and flippers.

Announcing the happy couple

At many weddings, the newlyweds are formally announced and presented to the assembled group. Everyone gets to their feet and applauds as you make a grand entrance.

This is your official introduction to society as husband and wife.

If you have this announcement at your reception, make sure you tell the MC what your names are. Some women change their surnames, and some don't ... and if he or she gets it wrong, there'll be a scene.

Wedding games

Some couples let the whole wedding thing go to their heads. Dizzy with being the centre of attention, they lose touch with reality and think they have complete licence to do whatever self-indulgent deeds tickle their romantic fancy.

Some examples I have seen with my own eyes are: a puppet show which re-enacted the romance of the bride and groom; a 20-minute video of the hilarity of the wedding rehearsal (bride and groom guffawing loudly, everyone else shifting uncomfortably in seats); some weird thing where funny quotes by the bride and groom were stuck under guests' chairs and we had to read them out to the people at our table; then there was the big performance of the blindfolded bride and groom trying to spoon dessert into each other's mouths.

What *were* they thinking?

I have a mate who swears that, at his cousin's wedding, the bride and groom played a bizarre version of the old swimming pool game Marco Polo, where the groom was blindfolded and he had to find his bride who was running around all the tables yelling out, 'Come get me, husband! Over here, husband!'

There should be laws about this sort of stuff.

Or at least, harsh punishments.

Speeches

More people are scared of public speaking than they are of dying. And with some of the wedding speeches I've heard, I can understand why.

The traditional format for speeches and toasts in years past has been quite specific and, let's be honest, sexist. First the bride's father said a few words about the bride and then he toasted the happy couple.

Next the groom thanked the parents and anyone who helped out in some way and then he toasted the bridesmaids.

Finally the best man replied on behalf of the bridesmaids (are females unable to speak for themselves?) before making his own comments and reading out those oh-so-hilarious telegrams.

This strict format is antiquated, inappropriate and, hopefully, a thing of the past.

When it comes to speeches, you don't have to follow tradition. I have been to a wedding where there were no speeches and no toasts; another where any guest who felt so inclined could get up and say a few words; another where the bride and bridesmaid were the only ones to speak; and another where the bride and groom, their attendants and all four parents had a few words.

If you're having speeches and toasts, you have the flexibility to be unique. It may be that the best man is a buffoon on the microphone, but the chief bridesmaid is an accomplished public speaker. It may be that the father of the bride is a nervous wreck but the mother of the groom has been waiting for years to make her public debut.

Whatever you do, don't go overboard with the speeches. Your guests want to drink a toast to you and applaud whoever's paying, and that's about it. Be especially careful in attempting to thank every person who has played a part in your wedding. You will find that your guests get pretty bored after ten minutes of '…and thanks also to cousin Mike who vacuumed the church, Mitsy who hand-made all the candles on the tables, Jen's friend Veronica who did all the make-up with her two sisters Sally and Anne. Thanks to Bob and Davo who handed out programs at the church and to my Uncle Steve for lending us his Statesman for our wedding car…and where's Tony and Susan who flew all the way out from Cambridge?'

You're better off writing thankyou cards rather than trying to thank everybody.

The reading of telegrams

In years gone by, people who couldn't make it to a wedding sent their best wishes by carrier pigeon. But with the electronic age (and the invention of the infamous carrier pigeon rifle), this was replaced by the 'telegram'.

Even though no-one on the planet has sent a telegram for decades, the word 'telegram' has actually become synonymous for 'best wishes from friends and rellies who couldn't make it but they've sent this funny little poem with a bawdy punchline that they think should be read out at the wedding'.

Fortunately, the disjointed original telegram style of, 'Ted and Alice STOP Sorry I couldn't be there STOP Have a great day STOP When you get back to your room alone, don't STOP Love Max STOP' has been replaced with the more fluent read of emails, faxes and letters.

If you have someone reading 'telegrams', tell them to keep it brief (because they are totally meaningless to most of the people there) and to edit all the embarrassing smut, in-jokes and pathetic innuendo (because they're never funny).

By the way, do you know why a groom on his wedding day is like a basketball player…? Oh, never mind.

The cake

The tradition of the wedding cake is one of the most established and long-standing of all wedding traditions around the world. From the ancient Romans and Egyptians, to Iroquois Indians and South Pacific Islanders, many peoples and cultures have celebrated a wedding with the bride feeding cake to her husband.

By the 1600s in Europe, fruit and icing were thrown in to the mix and made into many small cakes for all the guests. A bizarre precursor of the modern food fight, the tradition was actually to throw the cakes at the bride, but this was soon stopped because of bruising and concussion.

The French made this childish ritual of the cake more sophisticated by encasing all the little cakes in a marzipan casing and then breaking it over the bride's head. Ah, those sophisticated French!

Fortunately, now the tradition is for one large cake, the main aim being to eat it rather than use it as a projectile. All the guests are offered a piece, supposedly so they can partake in the love of the bride and groom.

Strict tradition dictates that people who can't make it to your wedding are sent a piece so they can still be part of the celebration.

I'm not sure exactly how it is that you're supposed to transport a delicate slice of wedding cake to the other side of the planet in post-it package, but I'll leave that dilemma up to you.

The tradition is for a tiered sponge or rich fruit cake with royal-white marzipan icing and lots of frilly stuff on top — maybe a little plastic bride and groom holding hands in a heart-shaped archway.

However, as the main function of any cake is to be eaten, there's nothing to stop your wedding cake from being a single-layer chocolate mud cake with guava icing and a herd of plastic lemmings pouring over the precipice of the cake onto the plate below, or whatever other combination, shape or design takes your fancy.

Your local cake shop or patisserie will have a photo album of designs and prices of the cakes they offer, or you could get your great-aunt to do it. It is a truth universally acknowledged that great-aunts are the best wedding cake makers.

The 'cutting of the cake' is perhaps the ultimate wedding tradition. In no other field of human endeavour is such significance placed on the slicing of a foodstuff. The bride and groom hold the knife and cut into the cake together as a symbol of their unity and love. (Members of the armed forces often use a ceremonial sword to do the job, although rumour has it they have to draw blood before it can go back into its sheath.)

At this point in the proceedings, guests with cameras knock other guests unconscious as they clamber over tables and chairs and bodies to get right up close to the action.

The cake is sliced, the guests applaud, the flashes flash and the cake disappears to be dismembered. Then, all the pieces come out and sit untouched in coffee saucers for the rest of the night, because the guests are either dancing or absolutely full after their three-course meal. And besides, no-one likes marzipan icing anyway.

Many couples keep a tier of their cake for a special occasion, like a first anniversary or the christening of a child. However, don't be like dopey friends of mine who put one of their orange-cake tiers in a sealed container and opened it two years later only to find the cake had evolved into a mould colony like something out of a horror flick. Only fruitcake can be stored away...unless you have access to a cryogenics storage facility, in which case your cake will last 2000 years and Walt Disney will be able to enjoy a slice when they bring him back to life.

The bridal waltz

The words 'bridal waltz' inspire a bevy of romantic images. Young fiancées become breathless at the thought of twirling and sliding around the dance floor, mirrorball scattering a dazzling carpet of light around the room, guests observing their fairytale movements with reverent admiration. It is like something out of a dream.

However, most bridal waltzes I have seen resemble a nightmare more than anything else.

The problem is that a waltz is in 3/4 time — not the most common time signature in the world of contemporary music. Many couples have never waltzed before (and never will again), and so they end up looking embarrassed and awkward as they stumble over each other. It's even worse when you can actually hear them chanting 1-2-3, 1-2-3, 1-2-3 as they bump foreheads, knees and feet.

If you want to waltz at your wedding, fine, go ahead, but at least do yourself (and your guests) the favour of practising a bit beforehand so the two of you don't look like a spider trying to mate with a meringue.

The best wedding waltz I have seen was not a waltz at all, but rather a choreographed dance to some groovy music. I'm still looking forward to the day when I see newlyweds do the lambada — 'the Forbidden Dance'.

Presents for the guests

It is likely that many people will make some sort of contribution to your wedding day, and good manners dictate that you thank them in some way.

Strict tradition suggests that personalised presents are appropriate. A book I read, for example, suggests tankards, tie-pins, watches and decanters for the best man and groomsmen, rings, stick-pins, thimbles, figurines and glasses for the bridesmaids, engraved platters and silver decanters for the parents, CD vouchers, wine and books for the ushers, musicians, drivers, cake decorators and other miscellaneous helpers, and even, for each other, a fur coat, string of pearls or a car for the bride, and gym membership, cufflinks or a motorbike for the groom.

Personally, I find all this elaborate present-giving a little excessive; surely you should be able to allow people the opportunity to contribute to your wedding without feeling the need to give them something in return? A pile of thankyou cards should be sufficient to show your gratitude.

And as for presents for each other, give me a break! As you've just spent more money on a single day than you ever will, and you've received a truckload of gifts, it strikes me as a tad self-indulgent to go out and buy each other pewter mugs. If you want to give your wife a present, have a shower before you go to bed that night, get a piece of red ribbon and tie a big bow on your...well, I'll leave the rest to your imagination.

Getting changed
When the end of the reception is nigh, some couples choose to get changed into 'going away clothes'. This is particularly appropriate if, for example, you are going straight to the airport and catching a non-stop flight to Zimbabwe.

This 'getting changed' ritual is no problem if you are in a home, where you can retire to the privacy of a bedroom or bathroom. If you're in a club or restaurant, however, pre-arrange a room of some sort so you don't have to striptease in the toilet with a whole lot of old drunk geezers standing at the urinal saying stuff like, 'Juss got married, didya? Ay? Geez mate, all brides are be-yoo-diful on their weddin' day and then they getcha home annay ged their claws inya...'

You may also want to make arrangements with your attendants to take away your clothes — i.e. returning a hired suit, or looking after the bridal outfit, which no doubt will need to be protected and packaged like a priceless museum piece.

On the other hand, you don't *have* to get changed. As it's probably the only time in your life you'll be wearing wedding get-up, you may want to maximise wearing time.

We stayed in our wedding gear and got a petty thrill out of driving through heavy traffic and arriving at the hotel in our full regalia.

The farewell
According to the strict rules of etiquette, it's rude for guests to leave the reception before the bride and groom.

This is fine, so long as the bride and groom leave at a reasonable hour. I'm sure you've been to weddings as a guest where, after a few hours, you've started looking at your watch and wondering if you'll ever get out.

For you as a newly married couple, however, it's a different story. When the sand runs out and it's time for you to depart, you can either do it quietly and quickly, or with fanfare.

If you want to leave without any fuss, wave as you head out the door with a 'thanks for coming, everyone...bye!'

But for many couples, their departure is the final ritual of the day (apart from that *other* more intimate ritual later on).

Often, this is announced by an MC ('Everyone, Brian and Cath are leaving now. Let's all give them a big farewell...') and may even involve the formation of a 'farewell circle'.

The farewell circle is where the guests form a giant ring and you and your bride walk around farewelling them all in turn. Your mates will say stuff like, 'Be thinking of you tonight, mate ... nudge, nudge,' while your bride will try to shake off her weepy, wedding-infatuated friends who have chosen this moment to tell her how much she means to them.

Throwing the garter/bouquet

Before you get out the door, don't be offended if some of your guests ask your bride to throw them some of her underwear.

In days gone by, the bride's garter was believed to possess sexual energy because it had been so intimately positioned up on her thigh. In throwing the garter to the single men present, she was bestowing her potency upon the lucky bloke who caught it.

... to throw them some of her underwear

(I saw one interesting variation of this ritual called 'throwing the beer can', which was hilarious to everyone except the guy who caught it. With his face.)

You've probably seen this debacle on those home-video shows where the bride throws her garter and starts a fiasco among the men which ends with blokes scattered like tenpins and tables getting smashed.

Garter throwing doesn't happen too much anymore, perhaps because brides began to question why they should make a public spectacle out of their underwear.

The flip side is the throwing of the bouquet to the single women present at the wedding, an action which is magically supposed to predict who will be the next to get married.

This can be quite a fun part of the proceedings, particularly if the bouquet hits a ceiling fan.

Driving off

The day is over. The service is done. The reception has come to an end. You've said your goodbyes.

All you have to do now is leave.

However, if you think it's just a matter of walking out the door, hopping in your car and driving off, then you've got another thing coming.

One of the most traditional of all traditions is the trashing of the married couple's car. Sure, this might have been funny when someone sticky-taped a 'Just Married' sign to the back window and tied a couple of shoes or tins to the bumper. But now you have to contend with more elaborate stupidity: the cabin filled with balloons, the steering wheel painted in peanut butter, confetti stuffed into the air-conditioning vents, the entire car wrapped in toilet paper, coins placed in the hub caps. Nastier tricks involve pouring milk under the car's carpets or hiding fish in the engine. I saw a bride reduced to tears when she and her bridal dress sat on a car seat covered in chocolate sauce.

My own car had its value reduced by $500 when my friends wrote messages all over it in shaving cream, which got etched into the duco. This doesn't sound too bad, but the car was only worth $600 in the first place.

So if you value your car, keep it away. Either catch a taxi or leave by more elaborate means, like chauffeured limo, a hot-air balloon or a horse and buggy. Alternatively, at the last minute, ask a trustworthy friend to drive you to where you have hidden your car a few blocks away, or pre-arrange with a friend to have them lend you their car.

And that's basically it.

All the little rituals out of the way.

The day is done.

Your car pulls away, accelerates, and you, with a final look out the rear window at your rapidly shrinking guests, are gone.

And suddenly it hits you.

After a day of non-stop talking and noise and music and activity, you are acutely aware of the silence. Your ears almost ring with it. And for the first time in what seems like forever, the two of you are alone. At last. No-one is looking at you. No-one wants to take your photo. No-one wants to shake your hand. You are no longer the centre of attention. You can stop smiling, relax, loosen your clothing and, best of all, actually talk to that person next to you who you now proudly call 'wife'.

At this point, you may experience any one of a number of emotions — relief, disappointment, joy, excitement, contentment, exhilaration, pride — and, of course, anticipation that in 30 minutes' time you will either be enjoying the embrace of your wife, or lying back with your mouth wide open and snoring like a steam-engine.

Organising the honeymoon

A hotel full of American golfers in checked pants? Well, at least it was memorable.

FIONA

Traditionally, newlywed couples head off on a private holiday called a honeymoon.

(Apparently the word 'honeymoon' came from the days when the bride's father gave the groom a present of mead, a wine made from honey, which the newlywed was supposed to drink during one cycle of the moon at the start of his marriage... or something like that.)

The honeymoon is the icing on the cake of the wedding circus. After all the excitement and tension and hectic activity, you're probably feeling emotionally, mentally and physically worn out. A holiday with your wife is just what you need.

The honeymoon is a time when there is nothing left to organise. It's a time when the most significant choice is between caesar salad or nachos. It is a time when you can turn your attention away from the calligraphy on name plates and turn your attention to relaxing, eating good food, recovering, talking, laughing, holding hands, sleeping in, ordering cocktails with slightly awkward and ambiguous names like 'Press me against the wall and give it to me hard', enjoying your wife's company and of course having leisurely newlywed honeymoon sex.

Your choice of honeymoon destination is bound by your budget, available time and personal taste. It doesn't really matter where you go, although I would suggest you get away rather than have a few days off and spend them in your house, otherwise all your friends will come over to look at your photos.

Whether it's a six-month European bus tour or a one-week hike through the mountains, a borrowed holiday house or a luxury resort on the beach, a caravan tour of Lower Estonia or a five-star hotel in the city, a white-water rafting adventure in the wilderness or a chalet in the snow, a tent in a paddock or a cabin in a winery, the main thing is that you relax, recover, enjoy each other's company and get used to being married.

If these things aren't proving possible, however, and you're having trouble relaxing, pause for a moment to consider the humble stunt-cyclist.

When a stunt-cyclist jumps over a row of buses (or a canyon or whatever), he has an enormous run-up. His bike gets faster and faster, and by the time it hits the ramp, the engine is screaming and he's travelling at incredible speed.

Then, *whoosh*...he's flying through the air.

At this particular moment, the rider is relying on the singular fact that there is a really long off-ramp on the other side on which to land and slow down.

Most married couples approach their wedding day like a stunt-cyclist. With a fully charged six-month lead up, they hit the day at top speed with their hearts pounding, minds racing and adrenaline pumping, and then *whoosh*, they're on their honeymoon.

Two of my friends left their reception at 2 am, got to their suite at 2.20 am and then left there at 6 am for an early flight. They flew halfway around the world, got severely jet-lagged, joined a whirlwind bus-tour ... and were genuinely surprised when they came back a week later (the night before they went back to work!) feeling cranky, tired, edgy, tense and reporting that there honeymoon was less than relaxing.

What did they expect? This is the equivalent of a stunt-cyclist landing on a ten-foot ramp with a brick wall at the end.

Be aware that it will take you a few days — maybe even weeks — to come down through the gears. Like the stunt-cyclist, you need a decent landing ramp on which to return to earth.

Many couples go to a nice hotel for a few days just to unwind before they go on their honeymoon proper. I think this is an excellent idea.

Meredith and I couldn't get a flight to our honeymoon resort until four days after our wedding. So we stayed in a nice hotel in the city, visited restaurants and art galleries, went shopping and swimming, slept a lot and basically got our feet back on the ground. When we flew out a few days later, we were refreshed and ready for a romantic island getaway.

However, as you start looking for honeymoon spots, tread carefully.

Hoteliers salivate at the sight of a honeymooning couple, because they know you are blind with love and stupid with romance and as a consequence are a ripe target for paying outrageous prices.

All hotels and resorts have wedding and honeymoon packages, which could include any combination of goodies like champagne on arrival, flowers in your room, chocolates, a gourmet hamper, monogrammed bathrobes, engraved glasses, free parking, continental breakfasts or a limousine transfer to the airport.

These sound wonderful and romantic, don't they? But before you go rushing off to make a booking, I strongly recommend you compare the package to the standard room rate. You're often better off taking your own bubbly and chocolates for a couple of bucks and using the money you save to go out to a great restaurant.

Wherever you go, have a memorable honeymoon. Enjoy it. Live it up. Drink cocktails. Swim in the pool. Sleep in. Take good photos. Submerse yourself in the depths of love.

I'll leave you with just three bits of advice:
1. Check the mini-bar price list before you hoe in.
2. Think ahead regarding food. Friends of mine went to a small island and didn't realise that the only food available was from the resort restaurant, which charged like a bull with a toreador impaled on its horns. They blew their budget pretty quickly and ended up eating bread rolls and potato chips from a vending machine.
3. Don't swap addresses with other honeymooning couples, cos you'll never, ever see them again. And if you do, it'll be awful.

6

The Big Day

(this is it)

'There is something surreal about your actual wedding day. It is the kind of momentous occasion that is rare in life. You spend so long looking forward to it and planning it and worrying about it, and then it arrives. You're in it and you're getting dressed. Before you know it you're saying the words you've being going over for sleepless nights and you suddenly realise that you are getting married. It's really happening.

Time flies when you're having fun, and ours flew by. There were people I didn't even say hello to. At one point, Danielle and I went into a back room and just sat down for five minutes alone and relaxed. We looked at each other and she said, "Hey, we're married" and we both laughed.
I'll always remember that.'

RAOUL, 38

Bucks' night

Yeah baby, get it off, get it off, get it off!
GARRY, TO 'BUBBLES'

I know a bucks' night doesn't actually happen on the big day itself, and in fact, only the most naïve groom would have a bucks' night anywhere near his wedding day. Nevertheless, the two do go hand in hand.

When a man commits himself legally to a woman, he says farewell to the Universal Brotherhood of Bachelors and signs up with the Fraternity of Married Men.

Most cultures mark this with a rite of passage.

A young man of the ancient Tenochtechtlan society proved his devotion to his woman by running a deer to ground, killing it and carrying it home to her on his shoulders.

A young man from Ichango in Tibet proves his devotion to his woman by making a night-time barefoot journey across the highest, bleakest, most treacherous mountain trails in the world to spend a night in an incense-filled sub-zero mud-brick hut, fasting and praying for his marriage.

A young man of the western world proves his devotion to his woman by getting drunk, going to a strip club to ogle a gyrating half-naked woman called Bam-Bam before having himself shaved, painted purple and chained to his fiancée's letterbox.

This is called a bucks' night (*aka* stag party).

Some people look upon the bucks' night as an antiquated ceremony of a bygone era — nothing more than a detestable display of nauseating machismo.

Others see it as a legitimate commemoration of the conclusion of one era of life and a celebration of the start of a new one.

For some it's a good night out with a few mates.

To others, it's a good excuse for a booze-up.

When the words 'bucks' night' start to pop up in your mates' conversations, you have three options:

1. Refuse to have one

It is not a foregone conclusion or a legal prerequisite to marriage that you have to have a bucks' night. There is no part in the marriage ceremony which goes, 'Did you, Eric, have a bucks' night? Did you drink till you spewed? Did you leer at girls and yell out "Woo-hoo! Hey baby! I'm getting married in two weeks …How about a little kiss?".'

You can stay home and watch telly instead.

It's up to you. I know plenty of guys who didn't have a bucks' night. Some didn't see the point. Some just couldn't be bothered. Others were simply scared of their best man, who declared that it would be 'a night to remember'.

If your mates are a pack of hard-drinking bozos who are going to do evil things to your body, this might be a good option. I'd rather tell my mates to get lost than end up chained naked to the roof of a car.

2. Go the whole hog

Both television and locker-room mythology portray a bucks' night as a yobboish night of drunken revelry where a pack of blokes wander blindly around the city looking for chicks, bars and fights till the sun comes up and the spewing begins.

This is fine…. if you're a drunken yobbo. Bars, strip-clubs and the local constabulary see guys like you every weekend.

If you do choose to do this, however, be aware of the consequences.

A few years ago I went on a pub-crawl bucks' night which ended in a brawl and, for an unlucky few, a night in casualty. A week later, the best man took the microphone at the reception and slurred his speech through a swollen face and a stitched upper lip.

If things get really bad, it could turn into one of those bucks' celebrations which end in the death of the groom. While I suspect that the 'Buck tied to roof of panel van which cartwheeled' is an urban myth, I remember the evening news horror only a few years ago about the groom who was thrown into the harbour by his mates and was consequently sent into another dimension by a passing propeller.

If you do choose to go out on a wild night, no matter what else you do, flick pass the whole stripper scenario.

On TV, strippers at bucks' nights are only doing it for the money to pay their way through doctoral study. They are elegant, tanned models who writhe seductively but tastefully in front of the groom.

I've been to functions with strippers and they are never like this.

I remember one particular cold, rainy bucks' where a woman appeared out of nowhere wearing nothing but a bikini and a feather boa. It was a strangely dissonant image in the context of the calm woody decor of the Thai restaurant in which we were sitting. The poor goose-pimpled woman jiggled about to the accompaniment of some poxy little tune dribbling out of a little tape deck, looking bored and humiliated. Most of us went back to arguing about the chronology of James Bond films. Then someone pinched her bum, she poured a drink down his back, slapped him and stormed out screaming that we were a bunch of stuck-up pigs.

Just thought I'd mention it.

And let's make it perfectly clear that any type of interlude with a prostitute is no way to endear yourself to your future wife. This is just not on. Your tonk is now reserved for her exclusive use. If you can't cope with that, you shouldn't be getting married.

Very soon you'll stand up in front of the world and declare your commitment, devotion and fidelity to your wife. Your words will sound a tad trite if, a week earlier, you'd mamboed with a paid woman while your mates hung around the door making noises like chimpanzees.

3. Opt for 'the noble male celebration' (NMC)

Your or your best man could organise an evening (or a weekend) that revolves around more than alcohol, naked women and being dumped 100 miles from home in nothing but a gorilla suit.

A bucks' night does not have to centre around larrikin antics. The essence of the event is to get together with your male friends to celebrate your impending marriage. It is a celebration of your manhood. It is a tribute to your future wife and your relationship. It is your mates expressing their joy at your impending marriage. It should be a positive occasion.

I have been to some terrific bucks' nights…. and they all had one common feature:

They were *well organised*.

Somebody — sometimes the groom, but more often than not the best man — went to the trouble of actually planning an afternoon or night (or both) of high-quality blokey activity.

If you're not very creative, here are a few suggestions for things you might like to do for you NMC bucks' night:

- book a private back room in a restaurant
- have a barbecue
- have a few rounds of an adventure sport: laser war games, paint ball, indoor rock climbing, abseiling, skid cars, etc. (note: alcohol, guns and heights do not mix)
- dress up as scouts and practice tying tourniquets
- organise a round of golf or a game of cricket, soccer or football
- go camping for a weekend
- have a surfing safari
- go to an amusement arcade or theme park

- play putt-putt golf or go tenpin bowling
- go boating, sailing or water-skiing (note: alcohol and large expanses of water do not mix)
- have a Jane Austen movie festival
- get waxed
- take a harbour cruise
- dress up as Elvis and see who can make the most money busking

The list is endless and is only limited by your finances, time, creativity, stamina and the average IQ of your mates.

I went to one epic bash which started with a lunch and a game of cricket. This was followed by several rounds at a pub and late dinner at a karaoke bar. The small hours of the morning were filled with pinball and snooker before the 4 am departure of the shark-hunting ferry for a few hours big-game fishing.

I only made it as far as the restaurant before flagging badly. There's only so much poorly sung 'Bohemian Rhapsody' a man can take before he needs to go home and have a good lie-down. But gee whiz, imagine how disappointed I was when I found out later that of the 26 blokes to make it onto the boat, 25 of them got seasick and vomited.

Another bucks' night I attended consisted of only me and two mates. We drank red wine as the sun went down, reminisced about old times, cooked a few steaks on the barbie and then sat around playing our guitars and singing three-part harmonies. It was one of the most memorable nights I've had.

Getting down to basics, a bucks' night is only as good as the people there. It's your mates who make it.

Here are my final five pointers:

1. Don't do anything stupid or dangerous that might get you injured or killed; don't do anything illegal where you might get arrested (the arrest itself might not be too bad, but you can bet that your father-in-law will drill you in his speech at the

reception); and don't do anything immoral which will compromise you or threaten your marriage.

2. Remain supportive and anonymous at other guy's bucks' nights. This reduces their desire for revenge.

3. Have your bucks' night two weeks prior to your wedding, thereby reducing the potential of vomiting during your vows. Also, it gives you enough time to regrow hair or to get back from some outback train station in another state.

4. No matter how funny it seems at the time, don't get a tattoo.

5. Take precautions, just in case. Assume that every person at your bucks' night will at some point get to see your underwear. So wear a clean and new pair, with good elastic. And sticky-tape a $50 bill to your groin in case you're stranded somewhere in you underpants and need to catch a taxi home.

On the day

*It was one of the best days of my life.
Unfortunately I don't remember much of it.*

MIGUEL

You wake up. There's a terrible taste in your mouth courtesy of the previous evening's 'last night as a single bloke wine and Indian food extravaganza', but that's nothing compared to the sinking feeling you have when you discover that your organ of creation has been shaved and tattooed with a smiley face.

Slowly the world comes into focus...as does your alarm clock, which you suddenly realise is telling you that you're getting married in 30 minutes.

You slept in!

You cut your face to ribbons in a hurried shave and bleed all over your shirt, which you don't have time to iron.

Eventually you get to Fragrant Garden for the service only to find that the grass has not been mowed and a swarm of bees has set up camp right in your spot. Your shoelaces are undone, your fly is down, some bozo has written H-E-L-P on the soles of your shoes and your best man tells you he left the ring at home.

Then the celebrant announces to your guests that she just had a call from the bride's dad: 'She won't be coming. It's all off; sorry. But they want you to go to the reception anyway. It's been paid for.'

You scream...and wake up.

Phew!

This is it.

The giant mahoonga.

Your wedding day.

Today, you're going to become a husband, tie the knot, get hitched.

D-Day...the culmination of all your planning and discussion and hopes and fights and dreams, whirlpooled into a few now-you-see-them-now-you-don't hours.

You've spent months climbing up the ladder to the diving board, and at last you're on the lip with your toes curling over the edge. Any second now you're going to jump off.

Head first.

Movies and jokes would have you believe that this is the moment when you stare deeply into the mirror-like surface of the pool and suddenly realise that it's all a big mistake, that you don't really want to get married after all, that you don't want to jump off the diving board. You don't love her. The only woman for you is that girl you sat next to in history class when you were 12 years old. You must go on a quest to find her...

Sure, in the history of marriages, there have been some that have been called off at the eleventh hour, but in reality most people would have worked through their pre-wedding jitters a while ago. I think you'll find you'll get up and experience nothing but excitement.

Today is a great day.

Your mission, should you choose to accept it, is to stand up before your friends and relatives and publicly declare your love and devotion to your wife; to legally join with her and create your own family unit; to take a step which will change the course of the rest of your life.

Today will be a day where at various points you may encounter anything on the spectrum of human emotion — melancholy, whimsy, hilarity, nerves, terror, disbelief, shock, sincerity, embarrassment, joy, ecstasy, pride, humility, gnashing of teeth and maybe even some tears.

And as you experience this roller coaster of emotion, I have two words of advice for you.

Enjoy yourself.

It seems stupid, I know, but on their wedding day a lot of married couples forget these simple words. They get the whole thing out of focus and the day becomes an entity in itself as they become subservient to chauffeurs, toasts, photographers and speeches. They spend the day looking at their watches and worrying if everybody is enjoying themselves. They keep their heads down, anticipating what comes next, and end up saying stuff like, 'It was all over so fast', 'It finished before it started' and 'I can't believe we spent so much money on something I can't remember'.

Don't get sucked into the minutiae of the day. Don't get fazed by the inevitable but ultimately insignificant bumps and problems. (I saw a bride go hysterical, once, because the table for the presents at the reception had been covered with a tablecloth of a different colour to the other tables in the room!)

Keep your eyes on the big picture.

In those defining and memorable moments when all your months of fantasy and thought and discussion come pounding into the real world like a giant waterfall and suddenly you're wearing a suit and you're standing there at the church or garden or synagogue or registry office or wherever…remember…*enjoy yourself.*

Soak up the atmosphere and relish your wedding day.

Look around you and take note of the sounds and smells and sights.

And whatever you do, don't get drunk. You want to remember your wedding clearly, not have second-hand reports of having vomited into a flower arrangement in the middle of your speech...

Okay, enough speechifying. You've got no time to be listening to me preaching. 'Cause you've got an important task at hand.

You've got to get dressed.

Scrub up

Well, how do I look?

EVERY BLOKE ON HIS WEDDING DAY

If you haven't noticed already, women and men have different behaviours in relation to personal grooming. Like the female Ossaway finch which spends its day preening its feathers (while its mate plays in dirty puddles), women have an elaborate 'getting ready' procedure.

They have a tonne of personal grooming stuff, most of which is beyond us blokes' comprehension — make-up, nail polish, jewellery, eye shadow, lip-gloss, hair colouring, a five-step protein pack, creams, gels, replenishers, cleansers, vitamin packs, solvents, fragrances, oils, powders, insect repellants.

And what have you got?

Deodorant and a razor.

When your fiancée's hair needs 'fixing', she spends a whole afternoon and half a week's wages at the swank chardonnay-swilling salon of some fellow called François. (He, apparently, is the *only* person in the entire world who can do her hair.)

And when *your* hair needs 'fixing'? Fifteen minutes and a few bucks at Vince's barbershop and you're looking sharp.

If your bride is an average bride — and I mean that in the nicest way — she will go to great lengths (and great costs) to look her best. Many brides see their wedding day as the one time in their life where they can go to town, no expenses spared, and spoil themselves rotten. TV and bridal magazines will have shoved the whole glamour thing down their throats, sprouting tripe about being 'radiant' and 'stunning' because 'all eyes' will be on them.

To illustrate the point, here's some advice from one bridal supplement in a local newspaper. In the months leading up to the wedding, the bride should:

- have cosmetic dentistry/tooth whitening ('Don't let an ugly smile spoil your photos!')
- visit an optometrist (to craft personalised contact lenses)
- find a personal trainer ('Fit into the dress of your dreams on your special day!')
- get advice from a jewellery and accessories consultant
- seek out a professional dressmaker
- obtain a personal florist

Then, in the days before the wedding, she should:

- have a leg/bikini line waxing
- book in for a facial
- have her eyebrows shaped
- get her eyelashes tinted
- have her hair coloured

And on the day, the article continues, she will require the undivided services of a professional:

- make-up artist
- hair-stylist
- manicurist/pedicurist
- masseur

Hopefully your bride won't be sucked in by all this extravagance. But even if she heeds only one-tenth of this advice and

... Vince's barber shop

spends only a small fortune (rather than a king's ransom) on her appearance, I bet you she'll look damn stunning.

So the least you can do is scrub up a bit. This is a special occasion, not just some afternoon on the driving range.

While I suspect you're not interested in fruit peels and podiatry, you should still aim to look your best.

If your skills in personal hygiene and presentation are lacking, here are a few pointers.

- Get your hair cut (and beard trimmed) a week before the wedding. You'll look slick, but it won't look like it's just been done. And if there's a haircut accident and your scone ends up looking like someone's run clippers around a fruit bowl, you've still got time to have a higher-level hairdressing professional do some necessary repairs.
- Don't eat garlic or chilli for 48 hours before your wedding.
- If you're wearing your own suit, have it dry-cleaned, and pick it up at least two days prior to the wedding.
- Clean and polish your shoes the day before the wedding. Shoe polish takes 24 hours to get out from under fingernails.

- Do all that stuff your mum used to tell you to: clean and cut your nails, use deodorant, brush your hair, clean your teeth (use floss), dig the sock-detritus out of your toenails.
- Shave. Use a new razor to give you that smooth and unhacked look.
- Don't go overboard with the aftershave. Be subtle. Women like subtle. Subtle is good.
- Put on new underwear, not those crappy old jocks with holes and bad elastic. If you've been wearing the same undies for a few years, invest in a new and more fashionable set. (Note: leopard skin is not acceptable.)
- Make sure your socks suit the rest of your outfit.
- Throw on some moisturiser and lip-balm, just for good luck.
- Have a good pair of sunnies. Sunnies are good. Sunnies make you look cooler than you really are. Except at night.
- Have a facial, but do it a week before your wedding. Facials open up all the pores and your skin takes a while to recover. A friend of mine had a facial the morning of his wedding, and in his wedding photos he looks like he's wearing a pizza on his face.

The rest of your marital preening is up to you, depending on your style and taste. I know guys who have bought special earrings for their wedding day, had a stint in a solarium to bronze up before their honeymoon (recommended if you want skin cancer), had a gym session and massage on the morning of their wedding, and changed the colour and style of their hair (this is not recommended). I even have one mate who went herbal and had a colonic irrigation. (Sorry, Mark, I know you told me in confidence, but it's just too good not to share.)

Murphy's Wedding

Julius: I think he's dead.
Kate: What do you mean 'dead'?
Julius: I mean dead.
Kate: Well this'll make for an interesting wedding.

'TEATIME BY THE SEA', E.B. JEFFERSON

In the countdown to your wedding day, you may have noticed the incessant and sinister pressure of expectation.

A wedding builds up a momentum of its own. It is not an isolated activity. It's a production, a saga, something that's months in the planning, filled with a cast of thousands and precipitating an overblown budget. It is an event, an unstoppable force, an immovable object, an intricate ballet of music and vows and speeches and cars and food and drink and flowers and bow ties and white frosted cakes with pink ribbons, all liberally sprinkled with nervous tension and romantic expectation.

A lot of work and money and talk and time and meetings and fittings and conversations and arguments (and, if you're unlucky, possibly even tears and yelling) have gone into this wedding. And so naturally everyone assumes and expects that all the careful planning of all the miniscule details will come to synchronised marital fruition in a memorable day, a fantastic day, a perfect day.

But let me reveal to you one of the most closely-guarded secrets of the wedding fraternity: your wedding day will not be a perfect day.

Take a moment to absorb this fact.

Yes, it will be *memorable*.

Yes, it will be *fantastic*.

And yes, it will hopefully be a day to remember for the rest of your life.

But your wedding day will not be *perfect*.

There are two reasons why your wedding day will fail to live up to your every expectation.

Firstly, people get precious about weddings.

There are often a lot of people who have invested time and energy and finance into this day. They've spent a lot of time planning little details, and they are anxious that everything will be just perfect. And when it isn't, look out!

I know one bride whose sister forgot to bring a pair of shoes for the bride to put on after the reception. She was so incensed, she yelled at her sister in front of all the guests and then sent her home to get them. As a consequence, the sister missed most of the reception... but at least the bride was looking after her feet.

I am often amazed how, on a day that is supposed to be celebratory and festive, people get so tense and abrupt and aggressive about stupid little things. They want everything to be just as they have fantasised and when something deviates from the plan, it seems like the end of the world. Nerves are on edge and if anyone in the bridal party is prone to violence or tears, you can bet this'll be the day to bring that particular personality trait to the fore.

Secondly, Murphy's Law. This undisputed law of universal socio-mechanics dictates that 'if something can go wrong, it will go wrong... and at the worst possible moment'.

Just ask Posh Spice and David Beckham, whose multi-million dollar wedding in an Irish Castle had to go on without Elton John (who was supposed to play their wedding dance) because he had the bad manners to have a heart attack instead. Or Jamie Packer, who discovered that even paying 10 million bucks for a wedding could not keep away the most torrential storm in living memory. Things weren't helped by a 4 kilometre limousine queue and a leaking $2 million marquee. Or consider the plight of Mark Bosnich, who spent the morning of his wedding being questioned by police over an altercation with a paparazzi photographer, forcing the ceremony to be postponed by an hour.

Four things went 'wrong' at my wedding.

1. It was the hottest summer day on record since the Paleolithic Era. Everyone was wet and limp and sweating. Make-up ran, shirts were drenched, someone fainted. Every man was desperate to lose his coat. This was not the weather of the perfect wedding.

2. Due to the aforementioned heatwave, we ran out of soft-drinks halfway through the reception. There was tea and coffee by the urnful, but no-one was interested. And so our guests had to queue up to drink from the taps in the kitchen and bathroom. I never saw *that* in any bridal magazine.

3. My meat-head friends wrote three giant words in shaving cream letters on my car. The shaving cream etched the duco and when I sold the car two years later, it still had 'Good one, Pete' clearly scrawled across the bonnet. This was not conducive to a highly profitable sale. I was not happy.

4. Due to a hasty loading of the camera, we brought a blank film home from our honeymoon.

I went to one wedding where the bride went to a park to have her photos taken and the photographer suggested she hold her dress out and run through the leaves, looking back over her shoulder for a classic bridal mag shot...which she promptly did, right up to the moment she was stopped by a tree.

I don't want to sound pessimistic, but there are actually a hundred-and-one things that might not go according to plan on your special day.

The minister might have double-booked. You might have a cold. The reception venue might have a power failure.

Some problems will be insignificant (even though, at the time, they will seem like cataclysmic events). The bride will run late. Your buttonholes will be the wrong colour. A relative will get on your nerves. The organist will play the wrong tune. The five-tier cake will fall over.

Other problems may be of more consequence. A bridesmaid will faint during the vows. Your father will have an anaphylactic reaction to the entrée and have to leave the reception. The best man will make a bad-taste joke about your last girlfriend during his speech, and the bride's mother will start crying. The hotel has no record of your reservation. You have a hideous cold sore, or ear infection, or whatever.

In all these situations, whether insignificant or more substantial, keep your cool. Keep your focus. Give your expectations for the day the flexibility to accommodate the bumps and hassles that will inevitably arise.

Remember what this day is all about. It's not a performance, it's not a spectacle. It's not about impressing anyone. It's about you and your wife declaring your commitment to each other.

So when you trip over your bride's dress on your way out of the church, when you fumble your vows, when the harbour cruiser arrives late, when the telegrams aren't funny, when a light aircraft crashes into your function centre, when Jesus returns through the clouds in a flaming chariot and you realise that the Bible was right after all, shrug your shoulders, laugh and remember that at the end of the day, you're married.

This advice will serve you well — that is, unless you encounter true tragedy. I have heard of two truly tragic weddings: one where the groom was killed at the reception by a firecracker, and another where the mother of the bride died during the bridal waltz. In situations like this, none of my twee advice will help.

There was also the one where the groom confronted his bride during the service about an illicit incident in the week prior, involving her and the best man, but I suspect that's an urban myth.

That first night

I'll just ... ah ... slip into something more comfortable.

ANY TV BRIDE ON HER WEDDING NIGHT

This chapter is about your first night together as man and wife, if you know what I mean.

But first, a note to my wife.

Meredith, if you are reading this, don't panic. I know what you're thinking: 'Oh no, Pete is going to reveal all sorts of personal stuff, just like he always does. It's so embarrassing. Why doesn't he learn some self-control?'

Well, have no fear. This one's between you and me. Private. Some things are sacred.

Except to say, *you were fantastic, baby!*

Ooops...sorry.

The first night of a newlywed couple is a long-standing cliché.

We've all heard jokes about the bride and groom on their first night, seen movies where the bride waits under the sheets with the expression of a rabbit caught in the headlights, heard wedding speeches where the best man jokes about the newlyweds leaving the reception 'because they've got better things to do'.

Hah, hah.

There is a certain expectation that the first night together as a married couple will be special: i.e. it will include sexual activity of the highest order.

This is understandable. You've just made the most important step and commitment of your life. It is appropriate to celebrate your love together and relish the fruits of what comes naturally.

The fact is, having sex with your wife is great. Not that I've had sex with *your* wife. I mean, I've never even met her... What I meant was, having sex with *any* wife is great. No, that's not right... What I'm trying to say is that sexual activity between a loving husband and wife is great.

Far better than a one-night stand or sex on the big screen, or fictional sex in the Letters to the Editor in men's magazines.

I'm talking about mind-numbingly tremendous sex. I'm talking about sex that transcends mere physical pleasure and reaches your heart. I'm talking about that deepest act of communion, that ballet of physical expression where the caverns of your soul spurt forth with torrents of...

Whoa... steady on!

When it comes to your first night as husband and wife, you will fall into one of three categories:

1. *The bloke who has already had sex with his wife.*

Whether you've lived with your fiancée for five years or just made good use of the back seat of your car, you have already driven the love bus with her on frequent occasions. So does this mean that the whole 'first night' scenario is still applicable to you?

Can it still be *special*?

Yes, *it can* — to an extent.

Sure, the element of discovery and surprise will be absent, but it will be your first time together *as husband and wife*. It is appropriate to celebrate this new era of your relationship together.

So when the two of you are finally alone after your hectic day and you close the door to your hotel suite, say some nice words

... sex ain't like you see it in the movies

about how much you love her and how glad you are that you've taken the big step of marriage. Read a poem and dim the lights. Then put on your Viking helmet, yell out 'For England, Harry and St George!' and go for it.

2. The bloke who has not had sex with his wife, but has had sex with other women.

You and your new wife might, for whatever reason, have refrained from doing the deed. Congratulations on your resolve. This will be a very special occasion.

Just one word of advice: don't give a post-coital comparative evaluation of your wife's performance.

3. The bloke who has not had sex with his wife — nor, for that matter, with any other woman.

You and/or your wife might be sexually inexperienced (as in virginal). If this is the case, your wedding night could fall anywhere on a scale between truly memorable and remarkably frightening. As a bloke with over ten years of premium-grade monogamous sex under his belt, let me tell you a few things worth knowing:

a) *Sex ain't like you see it in the movies.*

On the screen you see soft-focus shots of a man and woman writhing in choreographed ecstasy under satin sheets with candles burning and string quartets wafting in the background. Inevitably they'll have frantic simultaneous orgasms and then she'll lie with her head on his chest, twirling his chest hair in her forefinger. The two lovers always have bodies like Adonis and Aphrodite — he has a six-pack, and she, for some bizarre reason, finds it comfortable to wear a bra to bed.

This is crap.

Sure it's great, wonderful, (insert other appropriate erotic adjectives here), but those people are *acting*. They have directors and choreographers and people looking after their hair and make-up. Sometimes they even have body doubles. Their words are scripted, her breasts are silicone and an editor puts the whole thing together in the end anyway.

Having sex for the first time is like any new experience: you might be a bit clumsy to start, but you improve with practice. Think of the first time you hit a golf ball, or the first time you got behind the wheel of a car, or the first time you strummed a guitar. Some couples find their first sexual encounter awkward. Some find it embarrassing. Some find it painful. Some find it disappointing. Some find it the single most fantastic experience of their lives to date.

Don't get hung up about it. Take your time. Have a sense of humour and enjoy yourselves.

b) *Whatever you do, NEVER:*
- use another woman's name while whispering in her ear
- yawn
- ask if you can put a video on
- say, 'Are you finished yet?'

c) *You don't have to have sex on your wedding night.*

(To be honest, this was something I didn't even consider. A large part of my wedding day was spent counting down to the moment when the door would be shut behind Meredith and me at the hotel. But that's another story... and one you'll never hear.)

I know of one bride who freaked out on her wedding night. The pressure of expectation was too much for her. So her husband — whom I admire for his grace — spent the night in a different room. Luckily, Ed and Irene have sorted it out now. (Hi guys. Is it okay if I use your real names?)

I have heard other stories of brides being violently ill on their wedding night and grooms falling asleep in a drunken stupor.

Also, you could simply and literally be exhausted. You've been up since the crack of dawn and have spent the whole day on the hop as a bundle of nervous energy, smiling for photographers, making speeches and kissing relatives. It's the early hours of the morning and you've only just made it to your hotel.

d) *Sex gets better.*

Like many things in life, the more you do it, the better you get.

You come to learn each other's likes and dislikes, moods, temperaments and abilities to perform impossible acrobatic feats.

In the movies, it's only the young, beautiful and athletic who do the hoopy-hoopy nuddy dance, and the implication is that couples beyond the age of 25 are in their sexual twilight years.

Not so. Sex was pretty good when we started out, but after ten years' practice it's even better.

If we keep improving at this rate, we'll be sex-gods by the time we're 90... but that's not something I want to think about right now.

Part Two
Staying Married

7
Happily Ever After
(you hope ...)

'After we got married, we moved in together. Of course we got on well and enjoyed each other's company. But it was different.

Before we got married we used to see each other almost every night and every weekend. But it was always dinners, walks and going to the movies. And then we'd miss each other till the next time we were together.

But when you live together, someone has to take the bin out. You spend a lot of time just doing ordinary things. We had to learn to live with each other, and I had to learn that Michelle was not my mother.'

JACK, 21

The carnival is over

If men acted after marriage as they do during courtship, there would be fewer divorces — and more bankruptcies.

FRANCES RODMAN

In a well-publicised stunt in 1997, 144 couples got married at the Six Flags Theme Park in Wisconsin, USA. With the amusingly named Reverend Herring at the helm, the couples said their vows strapped into a carriage atop the 22-storey 'Giant Drop' ride.

You can imagine that they all probably felt on top of the world up there, dressed in their suits and white gowns, looking out at the majestic view and down upon all the little people scurrying about way below. Their hearts must have been pounding with the novelty and excitement of the occasion as they declared their love, perched there suspended in the sky.

And then, just as the fishy vicar finally pronounced them all husbands and wives, the ride was activated and they hurtled, no doubt screaming, at 100 kilometres an hour to the ground. In less than three seconds they had plummeted from the giddy heights of love. The ride was over and they were back on the earth amongst us mortals again.

This is very much like what happens when you get married.

You see, the whole wedding circus is, by its very nature, exciting and romantic.

For Meredith and I, the months leading up to our wedding were, despite all the hard work and the odd drama, rich with a sense of anticipation.

And after what seemed like forever, the big day arrived. What a day it was: early surf, getting dressed in a nice suit, a few celebratory ales, walking to the church, stomach churning with butterflies. The service was wonderful, Meredith looked delicious and the reception was terrific. We drove off together with everyone waving goodbye, and then, when we arrived at the hotel dressed in our wedding clothes, I got a petty kick out of saying, 'Room reservation for Mr and Mrs Downey'. We got up to our room and I walked towards Meredith and ... (THE FOLLOWING ANECDOTE HAS BEEN DELETED FROM THE TEXT AT THE REQUEST OF THE AUTHOR'S WIFE)... fell asleep in each other's arms amongst all the fruit, liqueur and ripped pillows.

A few days later, the romantic euphoria went into overdrive as we arrived for our honeymoon on an island in the South Pacific — a tropical paradise: sunsets, coconuts, men in skirts, relaxing by the pool, cocktails, duty-free shopping, the whole glass-bottom-boat-pig-in-a-pit-beach-volleyball-trivia-night-happy-hour tourist thing...

And then we came home and set up for our new life. We spent a week clearing 200 dinner invitations off our answering machine and then played with our wedding presents like kids on Christmas morning (it's amazing what you can do with a food processor, isn't it?), bought furniture and appliances, had friends over to 'our place' to see our photos. But the best part was just being together, deliriously married and waking up next to each other every morning.

Our life together had turned into one long, wonderful, romantic and exciting adventure.

But as the months went by, it started to change.

Our wedding day stopped being a conversation piece.

My wedding ring was no longer a novelty.

It no longer felt funny saying, 'And this is my wife, Meredith.'

And we got used to seeing each other at the end of every day.

Life settled into its inexorable routine: going to work, cooking dinner, washing socks, washing dishes, washing floors, doing the vacuuming, hanging the clothes out, mowing the lawns, grocery shopping, getting petrol, putting the bin out, making the bed, filling in tax forms, paying bills, yelling out from the shower, 'Will you bring me a towel?'

And so we discovered one of the great truths of marriage: the novelty does not last forever.

Like the couples on the Giant Drop, eventually you will find that the thrill of the ride is over and you have to come down from the clouds.

This is not to say that your marriage will never have romance or thrills again. Far from it! But candlelit dinners, poetry, roses and expensive presents wrapped in pretty bows cannot be the stuff of everyday life.

At some point the carnival will be over and your married life will begin.

And this is where the hard work begins — learning to live together, communicating, dealing with conflict, pursuing your goals, fighting for blankets in the middle of the night, raising children, managing your time and finances and roles, making major life decisions, being a loving and dedicated husband, trying not to use the last of the toilet paper so you don't have to replace the roll…

This is what marriage is all about.

You see, *getting* married is the easy part.

Being married and *staying* married are hard work.

But more of that in the following chapters.

Settling in

Women on average will speak 7000 words in a day; men, 2000. So many times when I come home, my wife swears I'm in a bad mood or I'm mad at her. Now I realise I'm just out of words. I've already done my 2000, she's got 5000 left.

ROB BECKER

Meredith and I were both living with our parents before we got married at age 21 and 24 respectively. (I had had a few experimental stints living out of home, but after months of eating only rice and beef satay sticks and sleeping on the same set of sheets, I returned to the relatively cheap and gastronomically superior abode of my parents.)

If until now you have only lived with your parents or by yourself, you've been king of your own domain, lord of your own roost.

You have spent *your* life doing things *your* way.

But when you cohabit, it takes a while to get used to living in close quarters with another person seven days a week. If you are already living with your fiancée, you know what I'm talking about.

We all have our own little habits and ways of doing things. and it can take a while to get used to each other's quirks, routines and idiosyncrasies.

I know one couple, for example, who went out together for years before they got married. They knew each other intimately and got on famously. Weeks into their marriage, however, they had a huge barney. It wasn't over money, or children, or chores. It was over a carrot.

They were in the kitchen making a stir-fry one night when the new husband started cutting the carrot into julienne strips. The new wife, however, said the carrot had to be cut into cross-sections, like small coins.

The ensuing heated conversation will not be printed here, but it basically boiled down to both parties saying, 'But this is the way I've always done it,' and, 'It's better *this* way.'

'How petty!' I hear you cry. 'I'm reading this book to get me ready for my marriage and I'm reading about fights over umbelliferous vegetables?'

Yes, yes, I know, it seems silly.

But it's often the little insignificant petty stupid things that are hard to deal with in a marriage.

To illustrate the point, here are some examples of the mundane minutiae that Meredith and I struggled with in our early days of learning to live together:

- I put wine glasses into the dishwasher. Meredith didn't.
- Meredith thought it was good manners to refill the icetray when you took the last cube. This had not occurred to me.
- I liked to sleep with the window wide open. Meredith liked it shut.
- Meredith liked to fall asleep while reading with the light on. I liked the dark.
- I wanted FM music on our bedside alarm clock. Meredith wanted AM talkback.
- Meredith hung shirts on the clothes line with pegs under the arms. I put the pegs on the tails.
- I wanted to hold the remote control while watching telly.

Meredith wanted to hold the remote control while watching telly.
- Meredith thought it was unhygienic of me to drink straight from the juice container in the fridge. I had always assumed that the cold would kill any germs.
- In bed at night, I'm a snuggly-wuggly person. Meredith is a 'get out of my personal space' person.

Some issues were resolved without a quibble (like squeezing the toothpaste tube from the bottom).

Some took a bit more work (like what items were acceptable for the compost; *well, meat decomposes, doesn't it?*).

Others issues continue to be problems, causing ongoing angst and frustration (like, for example, my wife's total and utter inability to put CDs back in their correct covers).

But knowing that there will be the odd bump along the way is to be halfway there in winning the battle.

With flexibility, maturity, a willingness to work it out, a good sense of humour, the wisdom of Solomon, the patience of someone who has lots of patience whose name eludes me at the moment, a realisation that you are not the centre of the universe and a recognition of the fact that there are bigger things in the world to be worried about, you will work through it all.

By the way, you will be pleased to know that after an extensive period of negotiation, Meredith and I compromised and we now cut our carrots diagonally.

Eye to eye 1: Not getting on

> *I knew I married Miss Right. It wasn't till later, though, that I found out her first name was 'Always'.*
>
> BEERMAT JOKE

Meredith and I always got on well. In fact, I secretly believed that our relationship was superior to all others. They all had their blues and sulking and tears and relational teetering.

But not us.

Never a raised voice or a harsh word, never a disagreement... except that time at the video store when Meredith chose *The African Queen* and I chose *Machine Gun Mamas: The bikini adventure*. The ensuing conflict was inevitable, but relatively minor.

Anyway, we never fought... until Day Three of our honeymoon when the immovable force met the unstoppable object.

You would, of course, imagine that after years of getting along fine, our honeymoon in a tropical paradise would be the ideal setting to continue in the general getting-along-fine vein.

But no.

You would also imagine that after years of getting along fine, it would take a cataclysmic event to send us over the falls into the turbulent whirlpool of marital conflict...you know, like me revealing to her that I had been married before and forgot to mention it, or her getting plastered during happy hour and spending all our traveller's cheques on a night of wild abandon on the poker machines with a tenpin bowler named Trevor. (For the record, neither of these events bear any semblance to reality.)

But again, no.

Our first tiff — and it was a doozy — was over a flash unit for a camera.

Yep, after years of coping with all sorts of stresses and strains, to say nothing of taking the whole wedding thing in our stride, our string of good times untwined over a little box that fits in the palm of your hand.

The escalating drama unfolded like this (to get the full effect, read faster and imagine both voices rising in pitch and volume as the argument proceeds):

ME: I think I'll buy a flash unit for the camera.

HER: What for? We'll never use it.

ME: Yeah we will. Let's get it now while it's tax-free. We'll need it sooner or later.

HER: No. It's *my* camera and we don't need one. There are a lot of more important things for us to be spending our money on.

ME: How can you not want a flash? Are you only ever going to take outdoor pictures during daylight hours? I'm getting one.

HER: No you're not.

ME: Yes I am, it's my money.

HER: It's *our* money.

ME: Oh I see, it's *our* money but it's *your* camera. Right.

HER: Right? What's *that* supposed to mean?

ME: What do you reckon?

HER: I don't know.

ME: Work it out.

I won't go on, but suffice it to say that the argument concluded with Meredith storming off to our room and me sulking off to the pool.

There I lay in the tropical midday sun, my mind spinning with disbelief and dire thoughts.

... honeymoon in a tropical paradise

Is this normal?
Is this a taste of things to come?
If we fight like this over something so insignificant, how will we go when faced with more important issues?
Does this mean Meredith won't be interested in sex tonight?

Fortunately, it was not a taste of things to come. And we have coped well with more important issues.

*Un*fortunately, Meredith was *not* interested in sex that night, so I moped around with my sunburn drinking beer and watching in-house videos while she read a book in bed.

Experience, anecdotal evidence and a simple knowledge of human psychology tell us that human conflict is, well... human. And so, marriage is not always the lovey-dovey tip-toe through the tulips that sepia wedding portraits would have you believe. More like sometimes you'll be stomping through your wife's flowerbed, crushing her tulips under your steel-capped boots while she flings fertiliser in your eyes.

In fact, a recent poll showed that out of ten married couples:

- three fought once a week
- two fought more than once a week

- one had disagreements on most days, and
- four were lying (or at the very least, deluded)

Just because you walk down an aisle and sign a piece of paper does not mean that you're suddenly endowed with magical conflict-avoidance properties.

So remember this: disagreements are normal.

Even the best marriages have them.

There will be times when your wife and you will not agree. There will be times when both of you will be angry or hurt, times when she will do things that will irritate you, times when she just can't believe that you are so obstinate, so stubborn, so damned difficult to live with, times when she is angry and sulky, and times when you can't understand what all the fuss is about. There will be times when you wish she was naked in the stocks in the middle of a shopping centre watched by television cameras and hundreds of people throwing rotten fruit at her and jeering and...ah, hang on, cancel that last bit.

I have a mate who has neighbours who fight every Friday night. They scream, slam doors, throw things, go out onto the street and swear at each other. It usually ends up with the wife calling the husband a sleazy drunk and the husband telling the neighbours at the top of his voice that his wife should get a job in a brothel.

In my experience, however, a lot of conflict is comprised not so much of screaming matches but of awkward silences and terse words. It comes not so much from big issues like me spending all my wages on the horses, but more from the stupid little things that are part and parcel of daily life. Like the other day when we were running late for a lunch and I had the engine running, waiting for Meredith to get in the car, and I took off before she shut the door. She thought I was rude. I was annoyed at her for dilly-dallying. So we exchanged a few short words and then sat and sulked.

Marital conflict can happen anywhere, anytime, over anything. According to one survey, disagreements over the following issues were reported by the following percentages of couples:

- children (51%)
- money (49%)
- ill-conceived responses to the question, 'Do these pants make me look fat?' (48%)
- chores (46%)
- relatives (45%)
- her lack of ability to use a road map (41%)
- social life (37%)
- toilet seat etiquette (33%)
- work (30%)
- use of the television remote control (27%)
- sex (26%)
- friends (24%)
- whose family to have lunch with on Christmas day (21%)
- the conflict between Sunday afternoon movies and weeding (15%)
- forgotten birthdays and anniversaries (9%)
- washing coloureds with white business shirts (7%)
- camera flashes (0.0001%).

'Yeah, well this is all well and good,' I hear you cry, 'but it's a bit theoretical, isn't it? Tell me something useful.'

All right, stop being so impatient.

After many years as a married bloke, I have come to the conclusion that there are *three types of marital conflict*. (Amazing — 200 years of psychology and I've distilled the rich tapestry of married life into three points!)

Conflict Type 1: 'I didn't see that coming'

Some conflicts in your marriage will be instantaneous and unexpected. No lead-up. No storm warning. They come out of nowhere and take you by surprise, like getting hit by a train when you're peacefully strolling through a tunnel.

One second everything's fine, but then one of you says something or does something, and suddenly you're wailing at each other like banshees. For example:

John forgets to go to the shops on the way home from work, and Chrissy's boss is arriving for dinner in 20 minutes. They have a yelling match.

At a dinner party, Angie makes a seemingly innocent joke about Simon's inadequacy in bed. He, however, is embarrassed, and he sulks for the rest of the night.

Briony is stuffing around with her hockey stick in the lounge room and knocks a glass of port onto Mark's laptop computer. He is cranky for the next two days.

After a hard day's work, Kay doesn't want to go to the movies. Ray says she's lost the sense of fun she once had. She is insulted.

Peter says he wants to buy a flash unit for the camera. Oh...I think you've heard that story.

These kinds of flare-ups are just par for the course on the fairway of life. It doesn't matter how hard you try, they'll happen to you too. Not because you don't love your wife. Not because you're cruel or nasty. Not because your relationship is in dire straits. It's simply that you and your wife are both human.

Conflict Type 2: 'You can't be serious'

When you are single, all of your opinions and ideas are valid. You are relatively free to please yourself, do your own thing and decide your own destiny. However, in a married relationship, the number of opinions in the air doubles. This is not even an issue most of the time. You actually deal with hundreds of these 'differences of opinion' every day. For example:

'Let's have spaghetti bolognaise for dinner.'

'No, let's have black pudding. I'm in the mood for an intestine filled with baked blood.'

'Yeah, all right.'

But, as I'm sure you're aware, some aspects of life are not so easily hurdled with a simple shrug of the shoulders. You will have to deal with many issues in your married life that have a significant impact on your relationship, lifestyle and family — often with serious and long-range consequences.

For example:

- Your wife has very high standards of tidiness. You think the best place for your stuff is on the floor.
- You desperately want to spend up big on new golf clubs. Your wife wants to save for a second car.
- Your wife is offered a promotion but it would involve moving interstate. You don't want to move.
- You want eight children. Your wife wants none.
- Your wife wants more sex. You're sick of sex.

These issues may go on for quite some time — days, weeks, months, maybe even years. Sometimes you will handle them in a mature manner in an attitude of mutual respect, love and consideration for your partner. There will be sincere and open discussion, and you will come to a point of agreement through negotiation and compromise.

Other times though you will handle your differences of opinion like toddlers fighting over the last piece of cake. There will be escalating tempers, sarcasm, raised voices, snide comments, accusations, innuendo, insults, sulking and cross-references back to things you did wrong two years ago.

Conflict Type 3: The 'exploding boil'

On a hiking trip once, I woke one morning with a swollen and sore knee. On close inspection, I noticed a tiny white spot there, about the size of the head of a pin. So I poised my thumbnails above the target, took aim and pressed down.

The next moments are kind of blurry, but I do remember a distinct cracking noise, followed by my tent-mates' screams of horror. The net effect of the aforementioned spot-squeezing has since been likened to a grenade going off in a bucket of custard.

Yep, I hit the king of abscesses. That misleading little pinprick looked innocent enough, but lurking under the surface brewed an angry, high-pressure fissure of virulent scrofula the size of a walnut.

You'll be pleased to know there is actually a point to this disgusting anecdote.

If an issue, disagreement or point of contention in a marriage is not adequately discussed and resolved, it may grow and fester. Everything may look fine on the surface, but underneath, that problem is getting worse.

Such problems usually reach crisis point with a niggly 'straw-that-breaks-the-camel's-back' comment or action.

For example, Ian watches TV while Beth brings the clothes in off the line. Later, he rushes dinner (which she's cooked) and goes out to the movies with his workmates, forgetting to thank Beth for cooking, and leaving her with the washing up. Two days later, he comes home from the gym and leaves his bag in the middle of the floor with a trail of dirty clothes spilling out, despite the fact that Beth has been tidying up because friends are coming over.

In isolation, none of these events may be of any particular consequence. But the cumulative effect is starting to chip away at Beth. She doesn't say anything, though, because she doesn't want to nag. Over the next few weeks, however, she starts to notice more and more little things that make her feel unappreciated and becomes aware of the fact that the workload in the house is unfairly shared.

One day she comes home tired from work (always a bad start) and, despite the fact that Ian said he was going to do some nice steaks on the barbecue for dinner, the kitchen is a mess, nothing's been done and he's sitting in the bath reading a book. He smiles and asks her to put the kettle on.

This is the last straw, and the only sound to be heard at this point is the severe snap of the camel's vertebrae.

To analyse this situation, aside from the obvious fact that Ian shouldn't have been such an insensitive slob in the first place, Beth should have voiced her concerns earlier on before things got out of hand.

Frank communication is important in a healthy marriage.

To conclude, disagreements are normal. You and your wife will not always see eye to eye on various issues. Sometimes you will make mistakes, sometimes you will say and do stupid things, sometimes you will be selfish and insensitive. Sometimes one or the other of you just won't engage your brain before you put your mouth into gear.

But that's okay. That just means you're human.

Ultimately, however, it doesn't really matter what the conflict is about. What matters is the way you deal with it.

But more of that in the next chapter.

Eye to eye 2: Working it out

All married couples should learn the art of battle as they should learn the art of making love. Good battle is objective and honest — never vicious and cruel. Good battle is healthy and constructive, and brings to a marriage the principle of equal partnership.

ANN LANDERS

Pick any topic or situation, and it is likely that a married couple has had a fight over it.

In the grand scheme, it doesn't really matter *what* you disagree about — like whether to have six children or six donuts — as much as *how* you disagree.

Your behaviour toward your wife should reflect the fact that, despite your differences of opinion, you are committed to the long-term good of your relationship and that you respect and love her.

Even when she's wrong.

According to one survey, the various behaviours in dealing with problems were reported by the following percentages of couples:

- harsh talk (83%)
- yelling (47%)
- sulking (47%)
- doing a monkey impression when the other person turns their back (32%)
- walking away (13%)
- challenging the other person to an arm wrestle (12%)
- throwing things (8%)
- denying 'sexual privileges' (7%)
- saying, 'Oh yeah? My dad could beat your dad' (6%)
- violence (2%)
- sprinkling itching powder in the other person's undies drawer (1%)

You will notice that none of the above behaviours are particularly conducive to solving the problem at hand. In fact, most of these actions would, if anything, exacerbate the problem …and maybe give you an itchy groin as well.

The ability to resolve conflict is a valuable skill. If you're someone who thinks 'because I say so' is a good way to resolve an issue, then the following pointers may be of some use to you.

Keep your focus

When you and your wife are having strong words over the fact that you were supposed to go out to dinner, but you didn't because she stayed back late at work, remember that your purpose is not 'to win' as if your relationship is some point-scoring competition. You're not trying to hurt her or belittle her or make yourself superior.

Your purpose is to deal with the issue under discussion.

So stick to it.

But if it looks like you're losing, tell her she needs to lose weight.

Don't expect miracles

Some conflicts can be sorted out quickly. ('Will you please STOP putting the peanut-butter knife in the margarine!')

But don't expect to solve all your relationship problems overnight. Some issues will take much longer to work through. ('Do you think we could have just one weekend *without* your parents visiting?')

If you disagree over your sexual relationship or leisure time or money, for example, it is unlikely it will be resolved with just one strongly worded conversation.

Use 'I' statements

We all have a natural tendency to be defensive when someone disagrees with us or is critical of us.

If you start a conversation (read: 'fight') with your wife in the words, 'You don't appreciate me ...', you're implying that the problem lies with her. So don't be surprised if she gets her back up.

Instead, re-word the same idea into an 'I' statement, like, 'Sometimes I feel unappreciated...'

It takes the accusation out of the equation and will tend to make her less defensive.

And once her defences are down you can really give her both barrels.

Just kidding.

Discuss the issue, not the person

De-personalise the issue. If there's something that your wife is doing that drives you nuts, don't criticise her as a person. Rather, target the action or behaviour that annoys you. For example, say:

- 'It's hard cleaning up this mess all the time' rather than 'You are the untidiest person on the face of the earth'
- 'I have a substantial libido and was kind of hoping that we might be able to engage in some sweet loving' rather than 'You're frigid'
- 'Let's spend a bit more time by ourselves' rather than 'You're insecure and your mum comes around too often'

- 'I feel we should keep a healthier buffer in our bank account for emergencies' rather than 'What is your problem with the credit card?'

Listen

It doesn't take a uni degree to work this one out. We live in a competitive world where individual rights are paramount and everybody wants to have their say and convince everyone else that they're right. But in the context of trying to resolve a disagreement with your wife, for a change why not keep your mouth shut and listen to what she is saying?

If you listen to what she says, and don't interrupt her when she is speaking, it will also encourage her to show you the same courtesy.

Know her style of dealing with conflict

We all have our own methods of dealing with conflict. *Your* method of dealing with conflict might not be the same as your *wife's* method of dealing with conflict.

It sounds simple enough, but this truism took me years to learn.

Meredith is an up-front person. She likes to work an issue through to the bitter end. She has a tenacious sense of what is right and what is wrong, a mind like a steel trap and the skills of one of those television lawyers who gets the defendant to confess to their hideous crime in the closing minutes of the show. If she was an animal, she'd be a bulldog.

I, on the other hand, tend to have little tolerance for conflict, instead defaulting to the 'Let's just forget it and have a cuddle' strategy. If I was an animal, I'd be a three-toed sloth.

The problem is that bulldogs kill three-toed sloths.

It took me a while to learn that when Meredith was standing in front of me with her arms folded and her teeth clenched because I went out for a beer after work and forgot to tell her I'd be home late, it was not ideal for me to reach out to her like a baby and say, 'Let's just have a huggy-wuggy.'

Avoid using the words 'never' and 'always'
Here's a typical argument between Meredith and me:
'Get off the computer. You're *always* on the computer.'
'Excuse me? I'm *always* on the computer? *Always*? I'm here all the time and *never* leave, is that it? I spend my life here, do I?'
'Well, no...'
'Why don't you cut me some slack. I *never* get to work without being interrupted.'
'What? *Never*? You *never* get to work without being interrupted? Even those times when I take the kids out for the afternoon?'
'Well, not *never*... but... often...'
'Why do you *always* say that?'
'I *always* say that, do I?'
You get the drift.

The problem is that 'never' and 'always' are words which, by their very nature, amplify any issue. And in reality we very rarely 'never' or 'always' do anything at all.

So, always remember never to use them.

Know when to postpone
When the entire extended family is sitting around the table having Christmas lunch and your wife makes a joke about how you're putting on weight, this is not the time for you to unload all your pent-up sensitivities about how she is always criticising you and how would you like it if your wife was always nag-nag-nagging about this and that and pass the turkey please you fat old...

In a situation like this, put the discussion on hold.

This is not to pretend that the problem doesn't exist in the hope that it will miraculously disappear. Rather, you are admitting that yes, there is an issue that needs to be dealt with, but no, now isn't the time to do it.

When you are exhausted after a bad day at work, you may be irritable and quick-tempered. Or if you've had a few too many drinks, you may say something that at the time seems honest but in the cold hard light of sobriety you realise was stupid and disastrous.

So wait until you are both thinking more clearly.

Don't think sex is a good way of sorting out conflict
It's not.

Learn to say 'sorry'
Statistically speaking, sometimes you will be in the wrong. In the heat of the moment it all seemed so clear, but half an hour later you realise that it was unreasonable of you to call your wife a lazy buzzard.

When you are in the wrong, admit it.

Apologise.

Wholeheartedly.

Don't ever apologise conditionally. Don't ever say, 'Look, I'm sorry…but sometimes you annoy me so much and blah blah blah…' If you say this, you're not sorry at all.

Be gracious
Statistically speaking, sometimes your wife will be in the wrong. In the heat of the moment it all seemed so clear to her, but half an hour later, she realises that it was unreasonable of her to call you a slimy weasel.

Hopefully she'll apologise.

Be gracious enough at that point to accept her apology and call it quits. Don't restart the argument to rub it in. Let the issue go and don't store it in your cerebral-argument-database for future use.

Communicate: clearly and calmly
A recent national survey revealed 'communication problems' to be the single biggest cause of divorce identified by both men and women.

So unless you want to be back in the singles market, you'd better start working on your communication skills.

Remember that everybody has disagreements, arguments or fights.

But if constant bad vibes, screaming matches, silences, aggro or coldness start dominating your relationship, you cross a line where you might need help to sort things out.

If you're swimming and you get into trouble, you don't wait till you're on the bottom of the ocean before you call out for help. Yet that's just what many couples do when they hit a rough patch in their marriage. They leave it and leave it and leave it and the problems worsen and fester and suddenly they're down with the seaweed. They should have called for assistance earlier on.

There is no shame in seeking the services of a professional counsellor. A counsellor can help the two of you to open up, explain your feelings, get to the root of problems and offer alternatives and solutions in a controlled and neutral environment. Many people come out of counselling sessions reporting a new awareness of their spouse and his or her feelings.

At the very least, it would not hurt you to read a good book on communicating or controlling your feelings.

... a new awareness of their spouse

Finally, remember this: you *will* stuff up. On re-reading my own pointers, I'm afraid I could probably give myself a barely acceptable score for being a good conflict resolver.

But I'm working at getting better.

And that should be your aim too.

So when your wife backs the car into a telegraph pole, when she throws out your collection of imported beer cans, when she spends your entire weekly pay on a new pair of shoes, take a deep breath, smile and tell her that nothing can shake your love for her.

Then go into a quiet room and bang your head against the wall until you feel better.

Honey, I bought you some roses ...

In late-breaking news, scientists have discovered a food source that reduces a woman's sexual impulses by 82%. It's called 'wedding cake'.

BEERMAT JOKE

Just before I got married, a work colleague and I had an afternoon beer. The main topic of conversation was, of course, my upcoming wedding.

We talked about stubborn in-laws, suit hire and wouldn't-it-be-simpler-if-you-could-just-get-married-and-all-go-to-a-nice-restaurant, etc.

Then he said something interesting.

Disturbing, almost.

He said that he and his wife worked hard to maintain a good sexual relationship. They *spoke* about it, about their attitudes and likes and dislikes. They put effort into their sexual relationship. They set aside time for it. Sometimes they even *planned* it.

What?

Talking about sex?

Working hard at it...like it's a *chore*?
Making an *appointment*...for *sex*?

I found this hard to believe. (After all, she was a nurse and every afternoon she came home wearing her uniform... But I digress).

Call me naïve, call me stupid, but I thought that when I walked down the aisle, the sexual floodgates would open and rampagingly great sex would be part and parcel of my daily routine.

Fortunately, when I walked down the aisle, the sexual floodgates did open and rampagingly great sex was part and parcel of my daily routine.

But now I've been married ten years.

I'm not going to go into personal details, because I know my parents are going to read this book. (*Hi Mum and Dad. By the way, when I was 14, it was me who scratched the car, not Jeremy*.)

Ten years on and I have discovered that my mate was right. A good long-term marital sexual relationship requires attention. Hard work, even.

That's not to say that there's never any spontaneity or fun or passion. Far, far from it. (*Mum, stop reading, please. Just move on to the next chapter*.) But it can't be like that all the time.

Sex is a major cause of marital disagreements and problems, with 26% of couples reporting that it is a constant source of conflict. Sex, or the lack of it, can even be the cause of marital breakdown.

In short, sex can be a big issue.

As far as I can tell, there are two reasons for this:

1. Men are more keen for sex than women.

This is not the most politically correct statement I've ever made, but it's true. Just ask anybody. You see, in the brain there's a spot that manages sexual activity. It's like a sexual Mission Control. (Don't worry, I won't make any 'Houston, we're attempting re-entry' jokes.) When this spot is activated and the little electrical impulses start flowing, then it's on for young and old.

In a man's brain, this spot is hard-wired permanently to the 'on' position. It's part of his mental hardware. There is no 'off'. And so the man is willing, able and ready for sex, anywhere, anytime — in the car on the way home, on the breakfast table, under a desk, in front of the television, behind a tree at a family barbecue, at midnight, at lunch, when he's running late for work, inside the sarcophagus in a museum... anywhere, anytime.

All it takes is for his wife to give him the eye and he's tearing at his clothes.

Men do not get sick of sex. They do not tire. There is no point of saturation (well, at least after a brief recovery period, anyway...).

The unfortunate and rather tragic problem is that it takes two to tango... but your dancing partner doesn't have the same brain.

She thinks differently about sex.

This comes as a surprise to many men.

As teenagers, we see porno films and think that women are in a perpetually amorous state and all they do is hang around at home in shorts and a singlet waiting for the plumber to arrive and as soon as he says, 'Hey, lady, can you reach my shifting spanner,' it's on.

And when you're standing in a queue paying for petrol, waiting for the idiot in front to work out how to use his credit card, your eyes glance over the women's magazines with their cover articles all about orgasms and lingerie and romance and how to please your man and body chocolate and rekindling the flame and all that stuff, and you think, 'Hey, that's great. Maybe my wife is reading these magazines and I'm going to get a surprise when I get home? Better hurry!'

This, my friend, is a vain hope. These articles are read by teenage girls who wear black and go out to nightclubs and who are still trying to figure out what relationships are all about. If your wife has this magazine, she bought it for the Danish nut-loaf recipe.

Why?

Because her brain is different.

Her sexual Mission Control is not hard-wired like yours. Hers is a switch with 'off' as the default position.

This is not to say that it's 'off' all the time, but for sex to be on the menu, the switch must first be cajoled to the 'on' position. (As Jerry Seinfeld said, while men are sexually like firemen who are ready in two minutes to answer any sexual emergency, women are like fire, which is very exciting to be around but needs exactly the right conditions for it to occur.)

A woman's body and her behaviours and responses are more influenced by the cycle of hormones coursing through her bloodstream. Sometimes, the chemical cocktail will flick the switch to 'on'.

But it doesn't hurt for you to help things along with a bit of seduction and romance. The key elements are talking, laughing, spending time together, stroking, back rubs, relaxing, afternoon naps, a candlelit dinner (cooked by you), a scented bath, tequila slammers, boxer shorts with a strawberry print, etc.

One word of caution, however. Sometimes, your wife will initiate sex. This will occur either when you walk in the door after completing a triathlon, or in the closing two minutes of a tied grand final.

In both of these scenarios you may attempt to momentarily deflect her advances. But know that two minutes later when you indicate your readiness, she will no longer be in the mood. It is a tragically brief window of opportunity. Don't waste it. If you do, years later when you are having a heated discussion about how you 'always' seem to be the one to initiate sex and she is 'never' interested, she will say, 'Oh yeah? What about that time when you were watching the big game?'

2. *We change as we get older.*

Sure, we all start out the same. Young, vibrant, cash-poor, time-rich teenagers, groping each other on the doorstep and hoping desperately that Dad won't open the door with a cricket bat in his hand, squirming about in the back of your parents' car at the local 'spot', climbing in and out of bedroom windows at all hours of the night. It all starts out fun. Exciting, thrilling, passionate.

Years later you get married and the good stuff starts. Being devoted and in love and committed to one another, sharing and being intimate — oh, and of course naked — is fantastic. God was very clever to have thought the whole sex thing up.

But days turn into weeks into months into years. You get older. Work gets busier. You have less time. The mortgage looms over your heads. The kids are physically and emotionally draining. You are perpetually tired; always on the go, never relaxed. You take longer to recover from a game of squash and even start wearing cardigans. You take out private health insurance and on a Friday night like nothing more than Thai takeaway and a video. In short, you turn into your dad. (Don't be hassled. It's just part of life's rich tapestry.)

To be blunt, in this climate of mundane suburban regularity, 'good sex' can rapidly fade into oblivion. Sexual familiarity breeds sexual contempt, and if you're not careful you can get blasé about it.

As a result, some married men end up feeling flustered, confused and angry. Steve feels that he is always the one to initiate sex. Dave thinks his wife does not find him attractive. Lyndon wants to have sex more than his wife does. Dominic is confused because his wife swings between being passionate and distant. Bruno is hurt because no matter what he does by way of breakfast in bed or back rubs, his wife isn't interested and he feels like he's 'begging'.

These are all genuine issues and very real concerns.

But you are not destined to feel perpetually out of sorts and sexually disgruntled — not if you work at it.

You and your wife have to put an effort into maintaining a positive sexual relationship. To help you in this regard, here are a few thoughts that I made up this morning as I lay in bed (sulking because my marital advances had been rejected).

Remember that sex is important

As a starting point, give sex its due place.

Sex is a natural and normal part of a healthy husband-wife relationship. It is the means of giving and receiving pleasure and sharing with each other. It is a private and intimate act of communion and affection that physically expresses your love and commitment to each other.

Oh, and there's also that whole furthering-of-the-species thing as well. And if none of us have sex, the cockroaches will be the ruling species on earth within 100 years.

Have realistic expectations

I admit that I when I first got married I thought I'd walk in the door every evening to find my négligéed wife with a rose in her mouth and a glass of bourbon in her hand, beckoning me to pleasures and whispering that she wanted to help me forget the troubles of the day.

Didn't happen.

Many men have unrealistic expectations about sex; expectations that cannot be realised and which only lead to frustration and perhaps even bitterness.

Some men expect a certain quantity of sex each week: 'But Julie, that was this morning!'

Some men choose the most inappropriate times: 'C'mon Laura, take your gardening gloves off and come up to the house...'

Some men have a ridiculous opinion of their wife's abilities: 'What's wrong with you, Helga? Most women have five orgasms in a row.'

Some men lack sensitivity: 'Look, I know you've just come home from a 14-hour shift, but I have needs too, you know!'

And some men are just plain unreasonable: 'Please Jacqui, just once. I'm sure your netball team will be in it.'

In your quest for sexual fulfilment, develop expectations that are realistic — expectations built not on adolescent fantasy but rather on the hard pragmatism of real people living in a modern world with its demands and pressures.

Understand where the other person is coming from

Like Atticus said in *To Kill a Mockingbird*, it helps if you can put yourself into another person's shoes and see things through their eyes.

Women and men are different.

You may have heard the adage, for example, that *men have sex to feel close while women need to feel close to have sex*. This would explain why your wife will be unresponsive when you come in the door and say, 'Hi honey, I'm home. I got the contract. Phil phoned from overseas. Let's have sex right now.'

Or what about *men are turned on by sight, women by touch*? This would explain why it is that when she arrives home from work and takes her dress off, you immediately think that she's inviting you to take her right there, right then, and are genuinely surprised when she tells you to rack off because all she wants is a shower.

These differences are (anecdotally) evident everywhere. Man masturbates more than woman. Man fantasises more than woman. Man likes pornography and novelty more than woman. Man plays air-guitar more than woman. When man meets woman, he stares at her eyes first (to be polite) and then her breasts (when she's not looking).

This is not some random mistake. There are actually reasons for these differences.

Biologically speaking, men have 1000% more testosterone than women, (which is the hormone responsible for sexual urges). This means that on a typical day she's operating on about 10% of your drive.

According to some researchers, men also have much more vasopressin (the hormone that controls blood pressure), which makes them more sexually persistent.

Anthropologically speaking, we are driven by instinctive urges which will assure the continuation of our blood line and species. The males of all species tend to be the sexual aggressors...except for those creepy female insects which do all the seducing then bite the male's head off.

Biology and anthropology aside, men have fragile egos and insecurities about the size of their organ of creation and therefore need constant reminders that '*Ooohhh, Kevin ... you're so big ... you make me feel so goooood ... mmmm ... take me, take me ...*'.

Be good at what you do

It may sound like I'm implying that all blokes are pathetic sexual beggars and women are cold, frigid receptacles who merely tolerate our advances. It may seem that I'm saying that sex is little more than a biological need, the relief of a pressure valve, an animal urge…

Not so.

A husband and wife should enjoy a healthy, satisfying and intimate sexual relationship.

Unfortunately, men have got a bad rep for their 'wham, bam, thank you, ma'am' approach to sex. They are criticised for being inconsiderate lovers.

It's time that we changed this perception. Your wife is not some sexual heat'n'eat snack. She is a three-course gourmet meal with expensive wine and cigars afterwards.

Strive to be a good lover. As author Rabbi Shmuley Boteach says, 'It's not the length of the stick, but the magic in the wand.'

So start practising your magic. It wouldn't hurt you, for example, to read a good book about passion, sex and love in marriage. There are plenty of relevant, funny and modern books on the shelves for you to choose from.

Get into a bit of mood setting, romantic talk, laughing and back rubs, and at all times remember the four most important ingredients of good sex:

No. 1: foreplay

No. 2: yep, foreplay

No. 3: you guessed it, foreplay, and

No. 4: films with sub-titles.

Talk

One of the most important elements of any relationship is communication. The process of exchanging ideas and thoughts and feelings and attitudes and opinions and likes and dislikes is absolutely central and integral and vital and essential and critical to the health of an open and positive and caring and warm and nurturing relationship and my apologies for using the word 'and' so many times in this sentence.

Don't assume that your wife is somehow going to guess your moods and magically perceive your every sexual whim and desire. Don't bottle up your frustrations. Don't fall into the trap of sulking or being self-absorbed.

It is important that you both speak openly about your sexual relationship. Listen to what she says, and tell her your likes and dislikes…unless you want her to stand in front of an open fridge before sex because you like her to be cold and clammy. Just keep that one to yourself.

Be affectionate

One criticism often levelled at men is that they are 'only affectionate when they want something'.

Fair cop.

A lot of blokes only ever buy flowers or cook dinner when they're expecting payback (i.e. sex).

So you can understand a wife being a tad on the cynical side. You can understand her exhaling heavily and thinking, 'Oh no, here we go again,' when her husband asks if she wants a foot massage.

Show your wife that you can be affectionate without it always meaning something else. You can cuddle and kiss and play and give presents and make compliments without it being an entrée to the main course.

Be flexible

Sometimes sex with your wife will be, to use the words of Goldilocks, 'just right'.

Everything will flow and you'll both be firing on all cylinders. You'll feel like Valentino on steroids as both of you writhe about in a wash of endorphins and other wonderful fluids and you get to that point where you feel that the top of your head has been peeled off and your brain is zooming off into the cosmos and you realise that your entire existence is all about this one single moment as you fall asleep in each other's arms totally delirious with love and affection.

But sometimes it won't be like this.

Sometimes you'll both be tired or one of you will be uninterested but tolerant. It'll be a bit half-hearted and clumsy and then you start thinking about what you have to do at work the next day and you both realise you're bored. You just kind of stop in a flaccid moment of disappointment.

This, too, is par for the course on the fairway of marital sex. Sometimes you'll get a hole in one, and other times your stroke will be off and you'll just stuff about causing a whole lot of divots.

Keep it in your daks

*Every man, whether he be young or old,
when meeting any woman, measures the
potentiality of sex between them.*

CHARLIE CHAPLIN

Recently I went to a holiday water park. The main attraction was aptly named 'Tower of Terror'. It was a giant waterslide, and I do not use the word 'giant' lightly. The staircase tower should have had a space shuttle on it.

Standing on the bottom step, I felt a mix of curiosity and fear, but in the end my sense of derring-do overcame my anxiety and I began the long ascent.

Fifteen minutes later — I had to stop several times, what with the nose bleeds and altitude sickness — I arrived at the top. Then the doubts set in. It was a long way up. And that, by a process of deduction, meant that it was a long way down. Just in front of me, my fellow sliders were disappearing into oblivion with ear-shattering screams.

The hairs on the back of my neck were less than happy.

Then I was at the front of the queue. The bronzed bloke working the gate looked at me and smiled as I clambered into position.

'First slide?' he asked.

'Yeah, how did you know?'

'You're not wearing a wetsuit.'

I turned to him, partly because it's polite to look at someone when you talk to them and partly because I didn't want to get vertigo.

'What's that got to...'

Then the gate opened and I fell forward. My entire stomach popped out of my mouth and inflated in front of my face. As I re-entered the earth's atmosphere, water sliced my face and pulled my eyelids up over the back of my head. Somewhere, someone was screaming, 'We're breaking up, Captain! We're breaking up!'

Random thoughts hammered my brain: *gravity, pain, water, wetsuits* and *midgets juggling eggplants*.

Then, splash-down.

Twenty minutes before, the pool at the bottom of the slide had looked cool and soft, but hitting it at the speed of sound it was like being machine-gunned by broken glass and razorblades. I aquaplaned across the surface, a blind 90 kilogram lump of screaming, tumbling flesh, feeling as if the world-champion tree-lopper had buried a double-edged axe into my buttocks.

I lay in the shallows flopping like a dying fish, my cossie ballooned up around my neck like a parachute. As I tried to get my eyes back into the front of my head, amongst the cheering and jeering of the crowd I heard a voice chuckle: 'Better get first aid.'

Yeah, bloody funny.

That's the attention-grabbing-anecdote-that-will-be-vaguely-referred-to-later-on out of the way. Now we can get to the hard stuff.

There's no simple way to go about spelling this out, so I'll just be blunt.

Lots of marriages are wrecked, ruined and indeed destroyed because blokes can't keep their daks zipped up. I'm not talking about forgetting to do your fly up after you've been to the whizzer. I'm talking about being unfaithful. I'm talking about putting your love truncheon in any place it's not supposed to go. No, not near a sandblaster or a pumpkin; what I mean is, near any woman who is not your wife

Sure, we can pretty it up with euphemisms like 'fling' or 'affair'. They don't sound too bad, do they? But that doesn't change what adultery is. It's having sex with another woman, breaking your promise to your wife and being unfaithful.

Sure, I know what you're thinking:

'Hey, that'll never happen to me. I'll be true till the day I die. I love [insert name here] and she's the only one for me. I would never do anything to hurt her. I'm not even going to finish reading this chapter as a sign of my contempt for this distasteful subject ...'

Well, good on you. I hope you *are* true and I hope you cling to your ideals tighter than anything.

But here's the rub.

For your first few years of marriage you will experience love and devotion that only comes from the security of commitment. Your wife will be like Aphrodite in your eyes and you'll count yourself the luckiest bloke on the planet. You'll wake up every morning and pinch yourself 'cos you can't believe she loves you and wants to spend the rest of her life with you.

But the years go by and the spark can dim.

Then, one day at work, an attractive colleague flirts with you. You're a 'happily married man', maybe by now even with a couple of kids. You have no intention of being unfaithful, but you find the repartee flattering. Nobody's fawned over you like that in quite a while. There's a stirring, but you think nothing of it.

You've just taken your first steps up to the top of the slippery slide.

Time goes by and the flirting continues and you start enjoying it more. Maybe it gets a bit stronger in intensity, more sexual. But there's no problem. It's not *an issue*. After all, you haven't done anything, right?

Clomp ... clomp ... clomp ...up the stairs you go.

... an attractive colleague flirts with you

You have lunch together a few times. And then comes a subtle brain shift. You occasionally find yourself thinking about her when she's not around. You start to notice her smell and her clothes and her hair. Maybe you start to dare to fantasise about *what it would be like.* After all, you're only *thinking* about it, you're not actually *doing* anything, right? And you never would anyway.

Even if you had the chance.

No way.

No harm done in just thinking.

Yeah.

Clomp, clomp, clomp ... Getting higher.

One day the two of you are the only ones in the office and you feel the thrill of taboo hanging in the air. Everything you say and do seems loaded with double entendre. It's exciting. You wonder if she's thinking what you're thinking.

You've reached the top of the steps and the slide is waiting there for you. You can hang around but it's only a matter of time ...

Later, when you go home, you feel a bit guilty. You love your wife without a shadow of a doubt. You have no intention of leaving her. And in the harsh light of day, you say to yourself that you'd never actually be unfaithful.

But a week later you're at a work dinner and your colleague offers to drop you home. You accept, a little too enthusiastically.

You sit into the slide with your legs dangling down.

Half an hour later the two of you are alone in her car. You've had a beer or seven.

You're hanging on with your fingertips.

It's dark. It's late. It's thrilling. You're stupid.

One hand lets go.

You're laughing. Leaning in close.

The other hand lets go.

Closer...

Whhhooooshhhhh. Bye-bye! You're down the slide.

I know at this moment you can't even contemplate the idea that this straying man could be you. But let's face it, it happens. Wandering eyes, unfaithful hearts, lying tongues and unzipped daks are responsible for about one in five marriage breakdowns. And it doesn't only happen to unhappy or sleazy guys. It happens to ordinary guys, fat guys, funny guys, guys with glasses, guys with bad ties, guys like King Frederick Augustus of Poland who had 345 illegitimate children, guys who start out their marriages with the same love and optimistic good intentions as you.

A bad-case scenario if you 'stumble' is that it will be a one-night once-only thing. You'll be lucky if your wife never finds out and instead you'll just have to live with your own guilt and remorse. You'll hopefully learn your lesson and never do it again.

A worse-case scenario is that it will be a one-night once-only thing AND your wife finds out and she feels like you've kicked her in the guts with a steel-capped boot. You do irreparable damage to your relationship and she never trusts you again, and every time you go out you have to report to her like a child. (If she does find out about your infidelity, you only have a 50% chance that your relationship will survive.)

But the really super-worst-case scenario is that your one-nighter turns into a two-nighter and then a three-nighter and then a six-monther and you then get tangled in 'a relationship'.

It's like going down that slide... but at the bottom, instead of cool blue water, there's the world's biggest collection of barbed wire. And it's electrified.

I read an article recently about a woman who discovered a phone number scribbled on a docket in her husband's bedside table and her investigations led to the discovery that he was having an affair. She thought their marriage could withstand it, but she was surprised to learn that he didn't really care about their marriage anymore. He was happy in his new relationship and just wanted out.

She was left pregnant, stunned and profoundly disappointed.

Don't be like that bastard guy.

Okay, so enough of the moral preaching. All this reads well on paper, but how do you stop yourself going down the slide of marital infidelity?

Well, here are some thoughts that might help:

- *Don't think yourself so high and mighty that it could never happen to you.*

Like the Scouts say, *be prepared*. If you're aware that you have the potential to stumble around with your daks down, then you're halfway there to preventing it from happening.

I have heard blokes express the sentiment that they were lucky that they found 'Miss Right', because she's the only woman on the planet for them. If they hadn't met her, they'd be single for ever.

What a load of crap.

The planet is literally teeming with women you *could* have married, and under different circumstances *would* have married. If you lived in a different city, or if one of you missed that bus where you first met, you may never have met. Like Gwyneth Paltrow in the movie 'Sliding Doors', your life would have taken a totally different course and you probably would have married someone else.

The thing is that these 'someone elses' are still out there.

At a function recently, I was introduced to an attractive woman my age, and I soon discovered that for 20 years we had both lived not 100 metres away from each other, but had never met. In one of those aforementioned 'sliding doors' moments it occurred to me that, under different circumstances (for example if I had gone to the shops one day and bumped into her), we might have struck up a friendship and then gone dating and eventually got married.

You might work with one of these 'alternative-reality loves' or live next door to one or meet one in a supermarket queue. Another time, another place and they'd be your wife.

But not this time.
And not this place.

There are plenty of women to be attracted to, but you've made your choice. And you're going to stick with it.

- *Regularly remind yourself of your vows to your wife.*

You made a promise to be faithful. It is a measure of your character as a man to live up to that promise. Remind yourself what you're on about in this relationship: commitment, trust, honour, love, sex and other good stuff like that.

I have a mate who rubs his thumb across his wedding band whenever he feels bad sexual vibes heading his way. It reminds him of his wedding day and his wife putting the ring on his finger, which quickly brings him back to reality from the other-woman flirtation danger-zone.

- *Watch the movie* Fatal Attraction.

Michael Douglas has an 'innocent night out' with a female colleague and, before he knows it, his naked buttocks are all over the screen. Soon she's running around his house with a big knife and boiling his family pets on the stove.

Watching this movie will make you limp around other women for the rest of your life.

- *Don't make excuses.*

I spoke to a guy once who had 'slept around a little bit' during the course of his marriage. His wife didn't know about it, and he considered that no harm was done. He said he 'couldn't help it' because he had a much greater sexual appetite than his wife. *It was a physical thing*, he said.

As far as excuses go, that's about as lame as you can get.

If you have a *physical thing* that requires a greater level of attention than your wife is delivering, can I suggest that you relieve the *physical thing* yourself, rather than bringing other people into the equation.

- *Play a game called 'consequences'.*

In Physics class at high school, I learned that every action has a consequence. (I fired a glob of tissue paper into the back of my teacher's head. *Believe me*, there were consequences.)

If you're in danger of messing with another woman, your brain is probably thinking in the short-term. It's almost as if the world will be over in 30 minutes and the most important things *at this moment* are flattery, the thrill of the chase, the excitement of breaking the rules and, of course, erotic pleasure. Nothing exists beyond that.

The game of consequences gets you to think past this event and into the long-term.

Let's suppose for a moment that you 'get with' another woman.

Now think through the consequences of your action.

What comes next?

For example, how would you feel after the deed? My guess is, the moment it was over you'd suddenly go, 'O-oh. Big mistake.'

Imagine the shame in your heart the next time you saw your wife. Imagine your disgust at yourself.

Imagine confessing to her what you'd done (or imagine her confronting you with her suspicions). What would be her reaction? How would *she* feel? How would *you* feel?

Imagine the tears, the anger, the bitterness, the hurt, the saucepans thrown at your head with the intent to kill or at least cause significant brain damage. Imagine the coldness in her eyes. Imagine your regret, your guilt, your stomach acid boring a hole through your body, your earnest desire that if only you could have your time again…

Imagine all your friends and family finding out about what you had done.

Imagine if she was so hurt and damaged that she went straight for the big gun — divorce. Life as you have happily known it would be instantly over. Your social circle would split. Your economic security would be shattered. Worst of all, you'd be cut off from the woman — and maybe even the children — you love.

Nice one, dummy.

You just traded a lifetime of fulfilling commitment for a few cheap thrills.

- *Put the shoe on the other foot.*

Imagine that one night your wife 'fessed up that while she was out on a girlfriend's hens' night a few months ago, she met this guy and they went back to his place and 'got together'. They've seen each other a few times since. Now she feels confused and wants some time to work it all out.

Imagine the sense of your world coming to an end. Imagine the knot in your stomach, the bitter taste of jealousy, the uncontrollable rage, the tortuous thoughts and images gnawing at your mind of your wife being intimate with another man.

Well, 'do unto others', pal.

- *Know the difference between fantasy and reality.*

All those Letters to the Editor in men's magazines — where happily married Joe Average has a sexual encounter with a busload of touring French hockey players — are crap.

As are all articles with titles like 'Have an affair and get away with it!' which in reality are written by fat old journos sitting in dingy offices drinking instant coffee and looking at internet porn.

There is nothing romantic or impressive about adultery.

- *Live by Paul Newman's edict.*

Why go out for burgers when you've got filet mignon at home?

To conclude, let's go back to the start of this chapter and my anecdote about the giant slide. What I was trying to say there was that the higher you climb, the harder it is to turn back. (You can quote me if you like.)

You see, once I was zooming down that slide, it was too late to stop. I had passed the point of no return.

I know a guy who left his wife for a woman whom he worked with. At first their relationship had been platonic, but bit by insidious bit they had got more entangled. After a while it had got out of control until eventually he was in love with this other woman and it was too late to turn back. By then it was too late to stop. Where he should have turned back, however, was that first moment he felt the twinge of attraction. He should have recognised it and killed it there and then before he took that first step.

It's important that you recognise your feelings, take responsibility for your actions and work out strategies to keep yourself in line.

Don't climb the staircase.

In fact, don't even put your foot on the first step.

Avoid situations that are going to escalate and be difficult to deal with. 'Cos the higher you climb, the harder it is to turn back.

And always remember that late-night drinks at the bar on an interstate business trip is like catching an elevator straight to the top of the slide.

The best things in life are free

'Money is indeed the most important thing in the world: all sound and successful personal morality should have this fact for its basis.'

GEORGE BERNARD SHAW

Money.

Some people religiously enter lotteries in the hope that they'll win it.

Some people risk their own on the horses in the hope they'll get more of it.

Some people steal and even kill so they can get their hands on somebody else's.

Some people need counselling because they don't know how to manage it.

Money gives us pretty well everything, from the biggies like a house in the suburbs, 5-star holidays in the mountains, a car with air and lambs-wool seat covers and a whoppin' great home entertainment system, to the little things like sour cream, video rental, bus tickets and deodorant. There's not much you can get without money.

Sure, it can't buy you happiness, peace or eternal salvation.

And, as the song says, it can't buy you love...unless you're a 93-year-old billionaire marrying a silicon-injected 20-year-old blonde with enormous gahoongas. (I know it's not technically 'love', but as if you'd care.)

Money gives us a certain independence, freedom and the ability to consume.

In addition, it introduces us to a world of headache and heartache.

In fact, 49% of couples claim to argue over the issue of money management in the home. It can be one of the most contentious issues within a marriage, providing hours of entertainment ranging from the odd mild disagreement to screaming matches. It's no surprise, if a marriage breaks down, that the division of wealth is one of the bitterest, longest and most savage battles... as well as a healthy source of lawyer income.

When you are a solo person (i.e. not married), you have total and utter control of your finances. You are Lord of the Stash, Master of the Treasury, Keeper of the Loot, Boss of the Booty. Your power over your own dough is ultimate and unquestionable. You can choose to horde it, invest it, spend it wisely, spend it stupidly, bury it and leave a map in an old book on Nordic architecture, or roll it up and smoke it (personally, I wouldn't recommend this; besides tasting horrible, it's illegal to destroy official tender).

Then your wedding day comes and goes and, all of a sudden, for the first time in your life, the rules change. Now your wife has keys to the treasury too. And you've got the keys to her treasury. You both stand there, eyeing each other up and down, wondering what to do about this whole two-treasury-two-keys situation.

When you get married, you are doing more than shacking up under the one roof. You are joining together *economically*. It's a company merger and, like a merger, there are bound to be a few adjustment issues along the way.

Many couples begin their marriages in a financially fragile state. The wedding day itself can be a significant drain on your resources, even if you're not bearing the full brunt of the costs yourself. And if you're not already living together, add to that the financial demands of trying to set up a new domicile. It's surprising how much a washing machine, cutlery set and lounge suite will knock you back, to say nothing of a cappuccino machine and a bar fridge. It's even worse if you're entering into the rental or mortgage market for the first time.

And then, just when you think it's all under control, a couple of unexpected bills roll in (new tyres for the car, telephone connection, insurance for all your new household goodies, damage bill for your bucks' car rally which went awry) and you feel the water level rising inexorably up and over your mouth.

Times like these, when the numbers going out are bigger than the numbers coming in, are when tempers can run hot and marital relations can be strained.

Add to this fragile situation the fact that you are no longer king of your financial castle. Sure, that's your name on the credit card in your wallet, but every night you climb into bed next to a person who wants to know what happened to that $200 you withdrew yesterday. (And similarly, when you find a $540 price tag in the bin, you're going to want to know where it came from.)

Like so many aspects of domestic existence, little things can mean a lot.

This first struck me a few weeks after Meredith and I got back from our honeymoon. It was a Friday night and I wanted to get Thai takeaway and a bottle of red. You know, some galangal soup, satay beef sticks, coriander green vegetables, and maybe grab a video with subtitles.

Meredith pointed out that we had only a handful of dollars left and it was another four days till either of us got paid and tomorrow she needed to buy a week's worth of bus and ferry tickets to get to work. On top of that, we had run dry on bread, milk and eggs, and besides, it would be kind of nice if any day now we bought a cupboard to hang our clothes in rather than having them dangling off all the doorknobs in the house.

It was the end of the week and I wanted to wind down, just like I did every other Friday night. And whereas a few weeks ago I would have been dialing the number on the menu stuck on the fridge, now I had someone saying, 'Now hold on there just a dang minute, young fella...'

And I didn't like it.

Even got a tad sulky, you might say.

As it turned out, in the long run Meredith and I have proved to be compatible in terms of patterns of spending and saving. We agree most of the time and the other times we discuss it and tolerate each other's little economic idiosyncrasies. (Personally, I think it's perfectly valid to buy a case of imported lager, but I still can't see why women's shoes are so bloody expensive.)

Ask yourself the questions and work through the issues.

How would you cope if your new wife didn't think about money in the same way as you? I'm not just talking about takeaway food and grocery items here. I'm talking about what you would do if you were a *saver* and your wife was a *spender*. In this corner is you, scraping every dollar together, investing it, watching it grow, budgeting carefully, saving for a rainy day, and in the other corner is your wife, who has no idea about money and who considers that if there's any in an account it's ripe for the picking to go out and buy whatever takes her fancy. Only one contestant will still be standing at the end of the round.

What if you've saved a bit and you want to spend it on an overseas holiday but your wife wants to spend it on a second car?

What if you buy everything on credit and have a massive and continual debt, but your wife is a strict 'pay-as-you-go' person?

By now you're probably starting to realise that part of being a good husband is being a good financial negotiator, manager and business partner.

I don't want to oversimplify the complexities of financial management, but for what it's worth, here are four ideas that might help:

Talk

It's no good just assuming that your financial management will look after itself. You have to discuss your financial attitudes and plans, both in the short-term and the long-term.

Don't wait till you're standing in a department store with your wife, who's got $500 worth of crappy Christmas presents for her nephews in one hand and a credit card in the other. That's not the time to start negotiating your familial financial management strategy.

Understand each other

Not everybody thinks and feels and operates like you in regard to money. But that doesn't make them wrong or stupid, or imply that you're better or smarter or anything like that. It just means that people are *different*.

I have two friends, for example, with very different attitudes to birthdays. She believes in buying expensive presents because that is the way she demonstrates her regard and affection. Her husband, however, thinks presents are just tokens and that they don't need to be extravagant. Neither of these attitudes are in themselves wrong, they are just different, and this couple had to learn to deal with their differences.

It is necessary that you come to terms with your wife's attitudes, and she with yours. You will need to negotiate and compromise. Because then she'll understand how come you just have to buy that Harley soft-tail.

Manage your accounts

The modern financial world is a lot more complex than in the days of *Little House on the Prairie*, where Pa would sell some produce and get a few coins and then give them to Ma, who would buy flour, salted ham and maybe some wool with which to darn socks.

When you get married you've got your own unique financial set-up — let's say you've got a workhorse bank account, a long-term deposit savings account, a credit card account and a car repayment account.

And your wife has her own baggage, too — an everyday account, a small business account, two credit cards and a mortgage.

But when it comes to the nitty-gritty of everyday money management, how exactly are you going to juggle it?

... presents are just tokens

When an electricity bill comes in, where will the money come from?

When the car's filling with petrol, who's got the cash?

When the waiter brings the cheque, who'll be reaching for the card?

Some couples stay totally independent and keep their own accounts and go 50/50 in everything. To my mind this is a bit complex, and kind of negates the whole purpose of getting married — i.e. to join together.

Meredith and I adopted the standard practice amongst our married peers and combined our economic forces. This has worked very well for us over the years. It saves a lot of fuss and is economically better in terms of fees and charges. Minor transactions occur all the time without discussion, but major expenditure or change of Downey economic policy is always negotiated.

Some of our friends have kept one account each on the side for a small bit of independent spending. Have a chat and work out what's good for you.

Budget

If you've already lived out of home for while, you can skip this section. (Just head off past GO and I'll see you in the next chapter.) But if marriage is your first venture away from your parents, this next bit is really quite important.

Here it is: budgeting means knowing how much money is coming in (wages, tips, book royalties, coins you find lying on the ground, estates left to you in a will, garage sale profits). Then you need to know how much money is going out:

a) *weekly* (groceries, rent/mortgage, petrol, beer, tithe payments, bus/train/ferry tickets, chocolate, entertainment)

b) *every so often* (gym membership, telephone, electricity, rates, gas, clothing, CDs, books, charity support, professional association, latest Star Wars CD-ROM, debt repayments)

c) *annually* (car rego, birthday presents, house insurance, car insurance, contents insurance, health insurance, comet-striking-the-earth insurance, provisional tax)

d) *savings and miscellany* (putting money away for rainy day or overseas trip, purchase of HomeGym Muscle Expander Plus from a late-night infomercial)

Comparing the two figures, the most important part is this: when you subtract the money going out from the money coming in, remember that a positive number is good, a negative number is bad.

The in-laws

*I like my own mother-in-law a lot. She's terrific.
And we get on well. Really.*

PETER DOWNEY

One day I met a genie who said, 'I'll grant you two wishes, but what I give to you, your mother-in-law will receive double.'

So I said, 'Give me a million dollars and beat me half to death.'

Boom boom.

The mother-in-law. There are internet sites devoted solely to this misunderstood maternal caricature, and hours of bar-room humour in her honour. No other person in the history of humankind, with the exception of Adolf Hitler, instils such fear and is the victim of so much stereotype. You can see her in your head now: a frumpy woman with clunky shoes and a Sunday-school teacher's handbag who goes around your home running her fingers over all surfaces testing for dust and commenting on the general grubbiness of your bath and the lack of fresh veggies in your fridge.

Before we go any further, you will be pleased to know that in my experience, and in my observations of friends' and relatives' families, this whole 'in-laws thing' is a myth. I know lots of 'in-laws', and aside from the obvious fact that nobody's perfect and we all have our failings, bad days and personality quirks, they are normal well-balanced people with their own lives.

Sure, some have a mother-in-law called 'the dragon'. But this is more a feature of her personality rather than being a characteristic of generic mother-in-lawdom.

Isn't this great news?

It *is* possible to like your in-laws and enjoy their company! It *is* possible for you to have interesting conversations and Christmas lunches that aren't tense and awkward! (On top of that, many mothers-in-law can bake cakes and knit jumpers like there's no tomorrow... *Oops*! There's that stereotype again.)

Having said that, at the start of their marriage, some newlyweds go through what we might politely call a 'readjustment stage' with their parents. And anecdotal evidence suggests that this applies equally to both bride and groom.

The issue arises, basically, over control.

See, the ritual of marriage is not only about starting a new life and a new family with a new partner, it's also about separating yourself from the old and 'leaving' your first family. Good parents spend their life educating and raising their child. The child is 'theirs' and they are in charge. The parents make their child's decisions, clean up their bodily fluids, control their finances, choose their clothes, pay their way, send them to bed and tell them what they can and can't do. For a large part of the child's life, their parents' authority is total.

Then, after a number of years have passed, on a certain day at a certain time the 'child' gets married. Even if you have already lived out of home for a while, when you marry there is the sense that you are signing up with another company.

For some parents (and for some of their offspring), this departure is easier said than done.

As a parent, it's a big step to see your baby move away from you (unless the 'baby' is fifty). It's hard to let go. As a result, some parents try to maintain their level of involvement.

They refer to this as 'just trying to help'.

Newlyweds refer to this as 'always interfering'.

During your courtship, your parents may disapprove of your partner or tell you you're too young to get married.

During your engagement they may annoy you with their ideas about guest lists, venues, speeches, choice of music, stationery and hire cars.

Then you get back from your honeymoon and the relationship with your parents changes again (unless they're like my dad, who, to this day has no qualms about clipping me over the ear in public).

Some newlyweds discover that their parents are more than happy to see the back of them at last.

Other parents, though, have trouble grasping the fact that you and your wife are not teeny boyfriend–girlfriend any more. I have heard of in-laws doing annoying things like popping in unexpectedly every day, or bringing around groceries and vegetables. I read one advice page where a new bride was complaining that whenever her mother visited she wandered around straightening pictures, fluffing cushions and putting clothes away.

Other couples complain of how their parents are all too keen to make under-the-breath comments, pass judgement and give advice on anything from the colour scheme in your flat to the way you carry your newborn baby: 'I hope you don't eat like this all the time', 'Now, sit down and tell me how you're going for money', 'I always find that if you do the washing up each night, you don't have to do it in the morning', 'It's a wonder you're not dead yet...'

I even met one couple recently who moved interstate to get away from the bride's obsessively interfering father, who didn't like his new son-in-law and made it his mission in life to criticise and pick fights with him.

These behaviours amount to territorial invasion and should be treated as such. You need to draw clear boundaries. This can be done simply by urinating on your doorstep.

If this fails, assure your parents that although there are undies left on the floor and you're using a milk crate for a kitchen table, your life is not falling apart.

Be firm. If they want to visit every day, explain in a loving way that you have left the nest and need some space to spend time alone with your new wife. If they persist, switch all your lights off at night and hide.

After a while, they'll get used to the new rules and everything will be hunky-dory...until you get to your first Christmas, when things turn really nasty as you try to work through the whole lunch-at-one-place-dinner-at-another-place-and-we'll-swap-next-year scenario, which is only slightly less terrible than after a few years when you declare that you're going to have your *own* Christmas celebration in your own home. That's when it really hits the fan.

By the way, what's an anagram of 'HITLER WOMAN'?

(Hint: It starts with the word 'MOTHER...'.)

Boom boom.

Cleaning the oven

A woman works her ass off all the time. The guy does two things around the house and he's got to show her. 'Honey, look! I fixed the screen! And look over there: I washed my dish!'

DIANE FORD

Now it's time for some reader participation. I'm going to go totally creative and ask you to do something.

Further down the page you'll read a word. As soon as you read that word, I want you to shut your eyes and free-associate it. What pictures or ideas does it bring to mind? What feelings and emotions does it produce?

I'm serious about this. Don't just skip on ahead. That'll spoil the fun.

Ready?

Okay, I'm trusting you to do it. Here is the word...

...on the very next line...

Wife.

(If you're still reading and haven't done the free-association thing, go back to the top of the page and start again!)

Now, store those thoughts for a moment and let's try it again, this time with a different word.

Ready? Here's the word...

Husband.

(Shut your eyes!)

Exercise over.

Here's the point. In the infinite recesses of your cerebral cortex, you carry around an entire library of conscious and subconscious baggage about what it means to be a 'wife' and a 'husband', baggage that you will carry into your marriage.

You have already formed certain expectations in regard to your wife and the role she will play in your relationship. And you also have certain ideas about your role as a husband.

When you shut your eyes, you might have thought about warmth and love, happiness and companionship, support and trust, long, slow, lingering sex, growing old together ... and all those other cheesy ingredients important to a healthy marital relationship.

But let's leave those to the side for a moment and talk about the nitty-gritty of married life, the nuts'n'bolts, the raw prawn, the stuff of everyday living.

Food will not magically appear on the table, shirts will not miraculously surface neatly ironed in the cupboard, and the porcelain bus will not supernaturally cleanse itself of your colonic detritus.

You and your wife have to work out how you're going to handle the business of life and the roles that you will play and the daily-grind duties you will perform in the home — and it is important that these ideas vaguely match up.

While I have no evidence to support this, most of your expectations about 'husband' and 'wife' have probably been set by observing the roles your *own* parents played in their marriage. This understanding may be vague if you were raised in a marital combat zone between two warring parents, or in a one-parent family without a live-in father/husband to model yourself on.

Let's say, for the sake of discussion, that your dad worked a five-day week, and when he came home he expected dinner to appear on the table before him. Activities like washing, cleaning, ironing and shopping were all the domain of your mother — who, curiously enough, also worked a full-time job. Your dad tinkered in the garage, mowed the lawns, trimmed the hedges and emptied the bins once a week. He was in charge of car rego, house insurance, the killing of spiders, tax and the changing of light globes, while your mum was in charge of paying bills. When you went on holidays, your dad drove the car and your mum made sandwiches and caramel slice. When you had a barbecue, your dad cooked and was in charge of 'music' and your mum made the salads and set the table. Your mum was a quiet, reserved person and your dad was a sit-at-the-head-of-the-table-and-deliver-edicts-about-life person.

As you grew up in this environment, you assumed that these husband and wife roles and behaviours were 'industry standard'.

But then you met the woman who would be your wife.

She grew up in a very different home, observing a different set of 'husband' and 'wife' roles. Her mum and dad both worked shift. Her dad did most of the cooking while her mum was a keen gardener who wouldn't let anyone else near the lawns. They both shared the washing up and cleaning. Ironing was done by whoever felt inclined to do it (including the kids, but generally it was the domain of her mum because she preferred her blouses without triangular iron-burns). The weekly grocery shopping was clearly the domain of her dad because he did the cooking, and besides, her mum was a shocking impulse buyer. Her parents had good conflict-resolution skills and often sat down to talk about important decisions that needed to be made.

So you and your wife waltz into your marriage with two very different ideas about what it means to be a 'husband' and a 'wife'.

Then, after a most excellent honeymoon, you soon settle into the world of work, chores and weekend leisure. One day you come home from work to find that your wife isn't getting dinner ready. She is surprised when she finds out you don't readily volunteer to do the weekly shopping. She does all the ironing one night but a few days later asks you to do 'a load' because she's busy scrubbing the bathroom floor.

Many couples begin their married lives in a state of shock as they struggle to balance their roles and align their expectations. In fact, almost half of all married couples report that delineation of roles is a contentious issue, causing fights and disagreements. This would explain why one radio announcer recently claimed that one in four divorces occurred over who does the dishes.

You and your wife have to work out your roles from scratch.

Start with a blank slate and divvy up the domestic routine equally. Leave your assumptions behind and talk through the most logical way for your home to operate. The division of labour should be fair and equitable. Your marriage is a partnership, and there's no room for you to be thinking that your wife is the unpaid help devoted to the furtherance of your leisure.

Sharing the domestic load doesn't mean that you have to draw up a spreadsheet with the days of the week along the top and 'chores' down the side, and a day-by-day 50/50 name allocation like you're at summer camp.

You can be flexible in your approach. Work, study commitments, finances, available time and maybe even personal preference will all play a part in determining who does what when. There will be times that require flexibility and one person doing more than the other, because of a work deadline or examination, but it should all work out fairly in the end. There might also be tasks that you take sole responsibility for, and others that get done on a whoever-feels-like-it basis. And you might, for example, hate shopping but not mind washing clothes, while your wife might find doing the ironing relaxing but cooking monotonous. Chat about how your home is going 'to work'.

To finish off, let's have some more reader participation. I'm going to go totally creative and ask you to do something.

I'm really serious about this. Don't just skip over it. That'll spoil the fun.

Ready?

With your right hand, reach across the top of your head and place your middle finger on your left ear lobe. Now, place the tip of your tongue up as far as it can go between your front bottom teeth and your lower lip. While still in this position, yell out the word 'cabbage' three times.

Hey, you better get a move on... there's a village somewhere missing its idiot!

525 600 minutes

*I have yet to hear a man ask for advice
on how to combine marriage and a career.*

GLORIA STEINEM

Mick Jagger once sang, 'Time…is on my side…yes, it is…'

Unfortunately, for the married man (and woman), this is not an accurate assessment.

Time is *not* on your side.

Unlike those long, hot summer days when you were a kid, time moves faster in the adult world of the twenty-first century, and there aren't enough hours in the day any more. Dinners with friends have to be booked seven weeks in advance. Our calendars and diaries and palm pilots are filled with commitments, appointments, meetings and functions. Our emails demand an instantaneous response and our mobile phones put us on call every minute of every day. Wholesome breakfasts have been replaced with energy bars and protein drinks that we eat on the run.

The 'leisure society' promised to us by technology has not delivered, and the world of work, with its many and various pressures, is busier and more demanding than ever.

Most people stumble through life in a perpetual state of going somewhere and doing something, complaining about how busy they are and desperately looking forward to their one holiday in the year when they escape to a cabin up the coast. (How many people do you know who ever say, 'Well, actually, life's pretty easy and I'm not doing too much at the moment'?)

For anything to turn out well, you have to invest time into it. Without time it is nothing. If you want to learn guitar, you have to spend time practising bar-chords and aeolian scales. If you want a magnificent garden, you have to spend time in it planting, weeding and covering the soil in horse manure.

Therefore, to look after your marriage, get a guitar and a horse and... um... hang on, I've confused myself... ah... where was I?

Oh, yeah...

Tragically, some married couples fail to grasp this simple but important concept. They get blasé about their marriage, don't make time for each other and get caught up in other things, often only passing like ships in the night.

Then they get divorced (the ship-in-the-night equivalent of hitting an iceberg).

Basically, part of being a good husband is learning to manage your time. In any given day there are 1440 minutes, and in a given week there are 10 080 minutes, and in a given year there are 525 600 minutes.

All those bits of time are a commodity and you have to work out how you are going to 'spend' them in juggling the many facets of your life without dropping any of the balls.

Some of your time will need to be devoted to *work*.

Living in our world is not cheap, what with the mortgage/rent, insurance, takeaway beef vindaloo, imported beers, weekly groceries, car repayments, computer golf software upgrades, taxation and anniversary presents.

Of course you need money to survive, but it's a fine line between working to live and living for work.

A recent international survey showed that the most highly prized goal of people in the modern business world was the ability to successfully balance work and family commitments. And yet, at the same time, about 30% of married couples report that they have disagreements over the issue of work, and 40% of men claim that their career significantly interferes with their home life.

It's up to the two of you to manage your work worlds and ensure that they support, not undermine, your marriage.

Some of your time will need to be devoted to *self*. It is important that you have space occasionally to recharge your personal batteries and listen to a CD or read a book or strum a guitar or weed a garden or catch a wave or knit a sweater or bench-press 120 kg (I wish!), and in doing so, remind yourself of who you are.

Some of your time will also need to be devoted to *mates*.

I am a great believer in the 'mateship' concept. Despite its lack of political correctness, I think it's important for you, every so often, to get together with your male confidants and do blokey things, whether that's having an ale or playing snooker or whacking a tennis ball or seeing a movie involving bloodshed.

It is important for you to have a few close mates who will support you in your marriage — blokes whom you respect, blokes with similar life ideals whom you can talk to about stuff and get advice from and have them say, 'Look mate, pull your head in and apologise to her…you're being unreasonable' rather than, 'She's like a millstone around yer neck, mate… Time to dump 'er and move on…'

Finally, some of your time will need to be devoted to your *wife* (and later on, maybe, your *children*).

You must spend time with your wife. You need to do stuff with her and see her and talk to her and be in her presence and listen to her and touch her and just hang out with her. That is the way relationships work.

A married relationship needs both *focus* time and *ordinary* time to survive.

Focus time is where you do things together and are focused on each other. It is when you are communicating, sharing, relating, talking, laughing, getting things off your chest, having golden moments... It is all those great memories that come from walks along the beach, going on holidays, having a meal together at the end of the day, going to the theatre, sitting in a spa drinking cocktails, having a chat over a coffee or setting aside a few hours for 'afternoon delight'.

Ordinary time is more mundane, but is equally as important. It is that deep sense of companionship, belonging and commitment that comes from living together and seeing each other regularly ... It is the cumulation of many insignificant moments doing the washing up, watching TV, sitting up in bed reading books, doing the grocery shopping, chopping vegetables or painting the bathroom.

Time management is an important skill.

Don't let time rule your life.

Be master of it, not slave to it.

Organise your life, your days, your weeks, your months, and make sure that your wife is a priority.

If you don't, you'll end up as one of those statistics who say, 'We woke up one morning and realised that we didn't even know each other any more.'

The patter of little feet

*One day I was a normal, carefree guy. The next day
I was driving a Tarago and wearing sandals and socks.*

PETER DOWNEY

I was guest speaker at a parenting conference a while ago and, as usual, I delivered my spiel of cute anecdotes, twee advice and offensive innuendo.

Afterwards, once the crowd had gone and there were only a few coffee-drinkers left milling around, I was approached by an attractive young woman with auburn hair and a bright red shirt.

She came up real close to me and, to my surprise, undid the top button of her shirt. Then she licked her upper lip and whispered, 'I've wanted to meet you for a long time, Peter...I was wondering if you might come back to my place where we can be alone. I want you to make me feel like a woman.'

Ha-ha. I was just testing to see if you were reading carefully.

There really *was* an attractive young woman, but what she said was a lot more tragic.

She explained to me that she had been married for eight years, and for the past four years had wanted to have children. Before they were married, she and her husband had only discussed parenting in a roundabout way. But once she started talking seriously, he started making excuses and putting it off.

Then, a few weeks ago, her husband declared that he did not want children... at all... ever. Not even one. He liked the way their lives were and he enjoyed their lifestyle and relationship. He didn't want anything to change.

No amount of discussion, persuasion or anger would sway him. They even had extensive family involvement, chats with friends and professional counselling. But to no avail.

He was adamant.

And she was devastated.

She became obsessed with her desire to have a baby. It was her purpose, a need integral to her existence. She really, really loved her husband ... but in her desperation had even considered divorcing him.

Here was this woman standing in front of me, absolutely ripped up inside, torn between her husband and her desire to be a mother. It was driving a very nasty wedge into their marriage.

The scary thing is that she is just one of 51% of married couples who argue over the issue of having children.

Not all people who are married want children.

Fine.

But for a large majority of married couples, having children is a logical and sequential step in their relationship. Marriage remains the dominant form of social arrangement for child-raising in our society.

You should cover this topic with your wife *before* you get married. You sure don't want any nasty surprises like the aforementioned woman got.

Statistically, odds are on that at some point in the next few years you will become a parent. For Meredith and I, this happened less than two years after we walked down the aisle. (Being young and stupid, we thought that getting pregnant would be difficult. Only in retrospect did we discover that we are as fertile as the Egyptian flood plain.) At the other extreme, a mate of mine has just had his first child at the age of 51, after 15 years of marriage.

No matter what age you are or how long you've been married, becoming a parent is akin to being hit over the head with a semi-trailer. It is a life-changer in every sense of the word and, as with marriage, should not be entered into lightly.

... not all married people want children

As the father of three delightful children, here is some of the barbecue wisdom I have learned on my own journey as a dad:

- You never have enough money and there's never a 'convenient' time to become a parent.
- Having children will not fix or smooth over any marriage problems. If anything, they'll make them worse.
- You don't have to be a 'kid-person' to be a parent. (I'm living proof!)
- Any idiot with a working appendage can get his wife pregnant. Being a parent takes a lot more time and effort.
- No matter how many birth classes you go to and books you read, nothing can prepare you for the joy, exhilaration and horror of the birth.

- You will need a bigger home, a bigger car and a bigger bank account.
- Being a parent is time-consuming, expensive, frustrating... oh, but also very, very rewarding.
- Becoming a parent is harder than becoming a husband. It changes the roles in your household and your relationship with your wife. When you become a parent, you have to work harder at being a good husband.
- Parenting can change your sexual relationship — sometimes temporarily, sometimes permanently.
- Your 'old life' (late nights at the office, Friday afternoon drinks, weekend lunches and dinners, gym, tennis, footy, poker nights, video nights, sleep-ins, impromptu cinema outings) is harder to manage and maintain.
- You can't call yourself a parent until you've: driven a nappy pin up under your fingernail; had your suit coated in baby vomit; experienced a toddler tantrum in a crowded supermarket; picked up toddler crap with your bare fingers without flinching; done the chicken dance at a preschool concert; and had your young child walk in on you and your wife during a passionate encounter and ask you what you're doing.

When Meredith got pregnant, it is an understatement to say that the whole thing took us by surprise. We were young and the main problem was that neither of us knew anything about having or raising kids.

So I decided to read some good books on pregnancy, babies and parenting from a bloke's perspective. But I couldn't find any...so I wrote my own. (See the shameless plug at the back of this book.)

If you read my books on fatherhood, parenting will be easy and your life will be a wonderful journey of discovery and fulfilment, with every day full of wonder, pleasure and joy.

And if you believe that, you're even more stupid than I was.

Get real!

These are very confusing times. For the first time in history, a woman is expected to combine: intelligence with a sharp hairdo and a raised consciousness with high heels.

LYNDA BARRY

Many years ago, back when we lived in caves and still thought fire was a pretty clever discovery, men didn't expect very much from their partners — maybe just that they would keep them warm at night and bear the occasional child.

But as society developed, our expectations of our partners increased.

Now here we are, at the dawn of a new millennium in an age in which we allow scientists to muck about with the genetics of our food (which just goes to show you how stupid we are after all), and we expect more from our marriage partners than at any other point in history.

We walk down the aisle and look forward to a blissful future as if a wife is 'the answer' to some ultimate riddle of life, as if all our problems are over now that we're getting married and that life is about to enter a new dimension of fabulousness. In this world where so much emphasis is placed on 'self' — self-fulfilment, self-actualisation, self-saucing pudding — we expect our wives to meet all our needs: to be a perfect match, a confidante, a stimulating conversationalist, an expert lover, a gracious hostess, a gourmet cook, an agreeable companion, a brilliant economist, and to have the looks of a model and a sense of humour to boot.

Unfortunately, many newlyweds start their marriage in this romantic haze of ridiculously high hopes and infatuation, a state that counsellors and psychologists refer to not as *love* but as *limerance*. This is a state of goo-goo eyes and skipped heartbeats, where the new spouse is put on a pedestal. They do not have any character flaws. Their annoying habits are 'cute'. Any neuroses are ignored, and all bad-hair days are tolerated. As such, expectations upon the new spouse are at a peak level.

The problem is that the greater your expectations are from your wife and for your marriage, the harder it is for her to meet them. Or, to use a high-jump metaphor, the higher you set the bar, the less likely she is to make it over.

Limerance only lasts a few years at best, and the flame of passion is replaced by the friction of reality. The result is that you may be left feeling disappointed, frustrated, discontented. You'll believe your marriage is a failure and that your wife has not come up with the goods. So instead of gracefully sailing over the top of the bar, she'll end up banging her head on it and crashing to the ground in a heap.

It is important that, as a married man, you have realistic expectations of your wife. This way you will be much more likely to enjoy your marriage and judge it a success.

It's like when you go to the movies. One night you see a movie you haven't heard of before, and it turns out to be surprisingly enjoyable. A few weeks later you see a movie you've been waiting months for — one of those movies that broke all box-office records in its first weekend. You've read all the reviews, watched the crappy 'Making of…' special on TV, seen the cast and crew interviewed on '60 Minutes', chatted with your friends about it. You can't wait.

'This is going to be the best movie I've ever seen,' your brain hammers as the lights dim and the credits roll.

Two hours later you walk out of the cinema thinking that it was 'nothing to write home about'.

The difference in these two scenarios is your *expectations*. You didn't expect a life-changing experience from the first film and it ended up being pretty good. The second film was a letdown because you expected so much more from it.

It's the same with your marriage.

Come out of the romantic Hollywood clouds and get real about your marriage!

Your wife is a human. She has faults. She is not perfect. She does not know all the answers. Sometimes she will be tired, she will look unattractive, she will not want to have sex with you, she will disagree with you on various issues, she will annoy you, frustrate you, tease you, anger you, she will think your taste in clothes, movies and food is crap, she will say things you might not want to hear, she will forget to do something she said she would, she will say something that hurts your feelings, she will flirt with someone across the dinner table, she will not be funny, witty, entertaining or lively, she will not want to go with you to that work function, she will wash your best white cotton business shirt with a cheap red gym singlet which runs…

And all your wife's idiosyncracies and flaws that you were so oblivious to in your limerant state — the way she clicks her teeth when she wakes up, the fact that she can never find fifth gear, her hang-up about eating meat, that annoying whiny giggle she does, her propensity to tell white lies, and a hundred other small irritations — will become part of your daily life.

Fortunately (and hopefully), your marriage scales will be more than balanced by the countless great times and fantastic aspects of your lives and relationship together.

The current generation of newlyweds is more cautious about marriage and is walking the aisle only when ready, often after a 'test' period of living together. Having witnessed first-hand the generations of split families and high divorce rates, these couples are marrying with their eyes open and with fewer expectations of romantic fantasy. They have no desire to repeat the mistakes of the past.

So keep your expectations manageable, achievable and realistic. You live in the real world, not some clichéd home-loan commercial.

And before you get too cocky or condescending, remember that everything you have read in this chapter applies equally to *you* as it does to *her*.

This can actually work in your favour.

I always encourage my wife to look at me as being an insipid, mediocre and unreliable husband. That way, I'm always surpassing her expectations.

Happily ever after

Love is a thing that can never go wrong,
and I am Marie of Romania.

DOROTHY PARKER

'... And the Prince and the maiden got married and they lived happily ever after.'

So finished almost every bed-time fairytale read to us when we were kids.

It's no surprise, therefore, that when most fiancés hit their wedding day, they've got that 'happily ever after' look on their faces.

Every weekend, I see it in the photos printed in the bridal supplement of my local paper. Pages of gorgeous young things dressed up to the nines, grinning from ear to ear, clutching champagne flutes, bouquets and each other, captured forever on film on the happiest day of their lives. Their gleaming eyes are looking out at a lifetime of wedded bliss and true love in the land of 'happily ever after'.

Unfortunately, however, our parents failed to read us the sequels to those fairytales all those years ago. We never got the full story. You see, Cinderella endured the rest of her life in a lonely façade of a marriage because Prince Charming was always away on official business. The great beauty, Belle, was surprised to learn that her husband really was a beast after all, and he just moped around the castle all day watching cable sports and getting drunk. St George came home early from a dragon killing one night and found a half-naked blacksmith climbing out of his bedroom window. The handsome Prince woke up one morning and realised that while Sleeping Beauty was drop-dead gorgeous, they had nothing in common, and in reality she was a bit of an airhead.

Sadly, as we hit this last chapter we must face the unfortunate statistical fact that of all of you reading this book, some of your marriages will not be the happiest and some won't last. For one reason or another, probably incomprehensible to you now, there will be no 'happily ever after'. In fact, 8% of your marriages won't get past five years, 19% won't make it past ten years and 32% of you won't be having a twentieth anniversary. (Hopefully you'll last longer than Jerzy Sluckin, whose wife Kathryn announced her intention to divorce him before they left their wedding reception.)

But that doesn't mean you have to lie down and wait for the great cosmic marital roulette wheel to decide your destiny for you.

The most important question you gotta ask yourself, punk, is how many bullets have... oops, no, I mean, what are you going to do about it? What steps are you going to take to ensure that you don't end up a statistic with a chalk-line drawn around your marriage?

What I'm trying to say is this: *a good marriage does not happen by chance. It happens because you work to make it happen.*

Which reminds me of my mate, Con.

Con runs a very successful computing business. The walls of his offices are covered in gigantic inspirational posters. You know the ones; they have bold headings like TEAMWORK (under a photo of a group of blokes pulling a locomotive with a rope), and NEVER GIVE UP (breathtaking shot of a rock-climber dangling one-handed from an impossibly high overhang), and

PERSEVERENCE (a runner striding out across a desert). Other posters encourage his employees to TAKE THE CHALLENGE, PURSUE THE GOAL and display VISION, LEADERSHIP, COMMITMENT and DETERMINATION, each with a suitably impressive photograph. (I'm still trying to work out if it's just coincidence that ALWAYS GIVE YOUR BEST is on the toilet cubicle door.)

The point of all this is that Con's business has succeeded because he's worked hard at it. He has made it a priority in his life and worked like a Trojan on steroids to push his business to the top. He has shown leadership and determination and perseverance and all those other inspiring ideals from the posters that adorn his walls.

Unfortunately, however, after only three years, Con and his wife separated.

It's just not working, he said.

A few weeks after he had moved out, he was sitting in his office one day when it finally dawned on him that he and his wife had applied none of the principles from his beloved posters to their marriage. They had not given their best to each other. They had forgotten about teamwork and commitment and vision and, in the end, they had given up.

Eventually they got back together, and with a newfound awareness of how fragile their relationship was (as well as a good counsellor), they set about rebuilding it. You'll be pleased to know that that was eight years ago and now they're going strong.

Like I said, a good marriage does not happen by chance. It happens because you work to make it happen.

Of course, reading this makes marriage sound so bleak and difficult and onerous. It sounds like so much fuss and bother and work.

Well, sometimes it is... but so what? A lot of the time it's just great fun.

Marrying Meredith was the best thing I've ever done. Along with being a dad, I count my happy marriage as my greatest achievement and the source of the utmost fulfilment and contentment in my life.

Well, that's enough of that soppy crap.

I hope you've enjoyed reading this book and that it has given you some thoughts to ponder.

I've spent too long writing it and right now I'm going to run a bath, light some candles, open a bottle of red and go see if I can find Meredith.

So I'll leave you with one final thought: thinking your marriage 'will just look after itself' is like relying on your car to fill its own fuel tank.

Your car needs constant attention... and so does your wife.

So, service her on a regular basis. Give her a wash and oil change. Lift her hood, check the dipstick and grease-nipples, test her shock absorbers and don't forget to fill her tank at least once a week.

Epilogue: Throwim way leg

*A teacher can open the door,
but you must enter by yourself.*

CHINESE PROVERB

A few years ago, my wife hiked the treacherous and infamous Kokoda Track in New Guinea.

At a small airstrip high in the mountains, she and her companions put on their weighty backpacks and stood at the start of the track, which disappeared into the dense undergrowth. In the distance she could see the mountain ranges that they would cross in the coming days.

It was to be a long and hard journey.

They looked at each other and one by one took the first step of their great adventure.

The people of New Guinea have a phrase for this. In Pidgin, 'throwim way leg' is the action of putting one leg in front of the other and taking the first step of a long journey.

And my guess is, that is where you are now — not at an airstrip in New Guinea, but about to take the first steps of your marital journey.

So I suppose now's as good a time as any to let you in on a little secret. I'm sorry to be the one to break it to you, but even though you have read this book, you do *not* know everything a bloke needs to know about marriage. And neither do I. The title of this book is, alas, facetious.

You can read books and trawl magazines and surf web-sites and do marriage courses till the cows come home, and still you won't even scratch the surface of what you will need to know to survive the years ahead.

But that's the whole point. The challenge and fun of marriage is that you learn as you go along.

I won't lie to you. It's not always an easy road. There's no guarantee that there'll be no tough times ahead. In fact, it's the opposite... I guarantee you that you *will* encounter tough times. There are no shortcuts or detours or going around or under or over obstacles. Being married is about you and your wife being committed to putting your shoulders together and ploughing *through* the tough times.

If you look ahead, you see the trail littered with hazards and obstacles — family politics, budget balancing, decisions, discussions, planning, tiredness, disagreements and a never-ending list of things to do... and all this before you even say your vows. Then the climb gets harder — learning to live together, communicating, financial stress, establishing roles, arguments over silly things, in-laws, bad-hair days... And then, when a few years have passed and you think you've got the whole marriage thing down pat, your wife one day declares those small but significant words, 'I'm pregnant'. And if you thought getting married was a big deal, you ain't seen nothin' yet, pal! Having a child is a whole epic saga of its own... but I've run out of pages so you'll have to read about that in my other books.

So although this book is coming to a close, your marriage adventure is just about to begin. Take a breath, grit your teeth, make sure your shoelaces are done up good and tight, keep your eyes focused on your 50-year wedding anniversary, take your wife's hand and begin your journey. With dedication, hard work and a willingness to keep going, even when the climb is steep, you'll soon find your stride.

I wish you well on your journey. May you be a good husband and enjoy a long and fruitful marriage in which you lovingly serve your wife until death parts you.

Go on... off you go. There's a woman waiting for you. You can't stay in the safety of this book forever...

Throwim way leg, husband.

8
The Stuff at the Back
(endmatter)

'When I wrote this book, I had a whole lot of stuff left over that wouldn't fit anywhere else. So I chucked it all up the back and hoped that nobody would notice.'

PETER

What my mates had to say

This book is about the ordinary man's experience of marriage. But so far you've only heard my semi-conservative and anecdotal ramblings. So I asked a whole bunch of blokes to imagine they were standing around a barbecue with a beer in one hand and a pair of tongs (lovingly caressing a rack of ribs dripping in bourbon sauce) in the other.

I asked them to pretend that as we stood around that blazing backyard sacrificial altar of testosterone and singed flesh our topic of conversation was weddings and marriage and stuff like that.

So here, for your edification and entertainment, are their random and unrelated anecdotes, jokes, advice and irrelevant asides.

Adrian was 23 when he married Annie (eighteen). He has been married nine years and now has two kids.
We met when my wife was 14 and I was nearly nineteen. My friends called me 'cradle snatcher'.

I run my own business and we've definitely had our ups and downs.

The most important thing in marriage is compromise. If you can't compromise and really can't work it out, see a counsellor. In a tough time, we saw a counsellor on and off for a year. Our marriage is a whole lot better for it. Just make sure you choose the counsellor carefully.

Al married Cathy 18 years ago when he was 22 years old.
I work as a Minister in a church so I get to do lots of weddings from the other side. I can watch without too much emotional attachment, so here are some observations.

Don't think it's *your* wedding. It's the parents' wedding. They've been thinking about it for years. If you don't expect to have much of a say, then anything you get will be a bonus.

Also, I see people who spend thousands of dollars and hundreds of hours in planning something that lasts an afternoon, yet give no thought to the rest of their lives. I expect that if people gave more thought to their 50 years of marriage rather than their 50 minutes of wedding, we might not have a 50% divorce rate.

Baz just celebrated his 50th wedding anniversary to Helen.
There is no secret to a happy marriage. It just requires commitment, time and goodwill. But one thing that has helped is the fact that Helen and I balance each other. I like to hoard things and she likes to throw them away.

Bill has married over 50 people, but most of the time he's married to Sue.
I worked as an Anglican minister for many years. Our church had an old and attractive building, so many couples wanted to be married there.

Many couples had thought at length about the details of the wedding day but had given little thought to the consequences of marriage for life based on an exclusive commitment to one another. This was surprising in view of the dire statistics concerning divorce; though perhaps it goes part of the way to accounting for them.

Also, the marriage preparation course that we ran was invariably helpful in getting couples to think effectively about being married. I would strongly suggest that any couple considering marriage, in a church or otherwise, do a course as part of their preparation.

Finally, while not an infallible guide, I think genuine Christian belief and commitment give a greater chance of a successful marriage. This is not because of the innate qualities of the people involved — far from it. It is rather that practising Christians tend to have a more realistic view of their own faults and so enter marriage with their eyes open to some of the difficulties.

Chris married Mel when they still looked like they were both seventeen.

An exchange (partially based on a true story):

ME: What should I say in Pete's book about marriage?

HER: Tell them not to try and understand the opposite sex, just enjoy the mystery of it all.

ME: It certainly is a mystery.

HER: What?

ME: You are.

HER: I just want some understanding.

ME: I know how you feel.

HER: How can you know how I feel when you don't even understand the opposite sex?

ME: I give up!

Moral of the story: don't expect logic from your wife.

Darren married Simone 11 months ago when he was thirty.

I have just finished booking a surprise 'romantic' getaway for Anniversary #1. People say that we're still in the honeymoon period.

Mmmm...honeymoon period? This weekend we argued over the dishes, the bathroom, the kitchen, who was most busy and countless other life-and-death issues.

But I wouldn't change her for anything.

Dashel's wife is Rachel.

This is my second marriage. I'm not really happy with that, it's just something I have to accept. After the collapse of marriage #1, I decided to take a long break. It was a good idea. Lots of time to clear my head and live on my own.

I have just recently celebrated my first anniversary in marriage #2. I must say that while being single is good, married life is much, much better.

I made some mistakes in my first marriage but realised them too late.

I won't make those mistakes again.

Guy and Michelle married when they were 30, about four years ago.
Michelle and I were having a getaway at a seaside resort. The hotel was lovely, and the dinner in the flash restaurant was proceeding nicely when a waitress appeared with two glasses of champagne and a card that read, 'If you ask me now, I'll say yes, but I may not in the future.'

So I popped the question, and she duly said yes. I then thought I should ring Michelle's dad, just to make sure it was okay. Leaving her, I ducked off and rang her parents, then my parents, who said I must ring my grandmother, and before I knew it 20 minutes had whizzed by. Michelle, sitting alone in the restaurant, had to reassure the waitress that the proposal had actually worked, and that I hadn't done a runner.

At 24, Huon married Louise, also 24, and three years later they've just had their first child.
Having travelled overseas, living out of each other's pockets (mostly out of mine!), and then moving in together (much to my parents' disappointment), I realised I had found a top chick.

So why get married?

It wasn't because of the ring, which I lost a year later, nor because our parents felt I should be making more of a commitment.

I guess I'm a little old-fashioned. I want to spend the rest of my life with Lou and I'm proud of that. We wanted to get married and it didn't really matter what anyone else thought.

Ian and Beth married after six years living together.
From the word go, it was a life-long commitment. In the past, I have gone out of my way to shun tradition, so I was quite happy to leave things as they were. But I came to realise that

the wedding ceremony is an important part of bringing family and friends together. Rituals are a significant part of life.

We're both actors, so getting ready for our wedding day was like putting on a show, except this was real life. It was an important occasion and I was quite moved by it all.

The marriage certificate itself didn't change anything in terms of our commitment. When her parents come to stay, I still feel guilty when we go to bed and then I remember that we're married.

James met Jane ...
... at 7 pm. By 10.30 that night she was a patient in hospital. I spent the next two weeks visiting and watching her throw up, and then it was all over bar the shouting (at the bucks' night).

We were married next May, and our first year had Jane hospitalised some seven times for asthma. When we announced our wedding plans, I was told that I should promise to take her 'for better and for worse, in sickness and in sickness'.

It's been more than great, even when the 'for richer and for poorer' has taken a beating. Four sons and a missionary stint in Africa were not on the menu back then, but married life sure has been a great ride.

James and Sarah got married 13 years ago.
So you get married, you have some kids down the track, your gut starts extending itself past that point that you remember when you were 19 and on the beach trying to impress all those sun goddesses, you get grey hair and not just on your head, you start abusing P-plate drivers and you get tired about 9.30 pm every night. Basically, your life is shot. So why not be married?

Jason is getting married to Eileen any day now.
I am sitting in a transit lounge at 1 am on route to Cananda... and my wedding. It's all very exciting.

In the three years Eileen and I have known each other, we have never disagreed on so much as we have about our wedding day. Apparently, the linen on the guest book table is supposed to match the tablecloths, which complement the flowers, which set off the cake decorations, which provide a contrast to the boutonniere...I don't even know what a boutonniere is!

Even so, I can hardly wait to get married.

John married Chrissy almost ten years ago.
For me, the decision to get married was not easy. I only wanted to do it once, and I felt a lot of pressure to find 'the right girl'. The problem was, I didn't know who the right girl was.

At the time I thought that the key to a successful marriage was making sure I had found the most compatible girl possible. I have now changed my mind.

I still think that compatibility is important. However, I now know that the most important element of a good marriage is taking time to nurture the relationship. Chrissy and I try to find time each day to tune into each other — to find out about how the day has been and to hear about the ups and downs. We have had to learn to listen to each other, discuss differences and be prepared to compromise or give in to each other at times.

Each child (there are currently three of them) has made this harder to do, but all the more important. It hasn't always been easy, but I wouldn't have it any other way.

John (42), husband of Keiko (32). Married five years.
Supposedly, a Japanese wife will be dutifully devoted to your every need. I certainly got the exception.

Keiko is feisty, independent and totally egalitarian about all things domestic — and, more importantly, she is tolerant of my fast-approaching midlife crisis.

We both married relatively late in life and with a ten-year age difference. But we realise that at an earlier age neither of us was prepared for the demands and rigours of married life. With our long-held independence, our limited patience and our valued solitude, we probably would not have survived a month.

Today, after two wedding ceremonies and one beautiful baby girl, we have a highly unusual marriage based on mutual sharing, caring and respect — which, I might immodestly add, has seen me elevated to the status of 'husband number one' among her friends and associates.

Ken was 40 when he married Julie.

I've always been a 'sleeping-bag-on-the-floor' guy. Years of singleness saw me forsake the soft comfort of a bed and go to the sublime delight of a sleeping mat on the carpet. I grew to love that camping feeling as I crawled into my sleeping bag each night.

Then I got married and my nocturnal arrangements were thrown into chaos. I now live with mattresses and doonas, bed sheets and box springs, stuffed animals and quilt covers.

While there are obvious advantages to having a lovely bed partner, I'm having a hard time adjusting.

Each night these frozen extremities wrap themselves around the nearest part of my body seeking warmth and comfort.

But the feet are nothing compared to the great heat-seeking bum, which desperately needs to be placed against the small of my back throughout the whole night. No matter which way I turn, it seeks me out like an infra-red device.

There are other issues. Without fail, periodically it comes time for her to roll over. The arm comes out, the blankets go up, the manoeuvre is made and suddenly an icepick rips through our bed like some Arctic tornado. I used to sleep naked. Now I wear a beanie, T-shirt, tracksuit, socks, mittens, slippers…

Ah, the joys of married life…

Kevin, widowed husband of Margaret, now husband to Michele. Grand-dad of too many children to count.

Margaret and I were 22 and 24 when we were married. After 32 years of a very happy marriage, she was diagnosed with a cancer that would not respond to treatment.

It is one of the most traumatic things to watch your wife waste away and die, knowing there is nothing you can do. While family and friends can be a great support, the reality is that you have to get on with life. It can be very lonely sitting around in a big house by yourself cooking a single piece of steak for dinner every night.

A few years later, Michele and I were married. My family welcomed her openly and I was proud to have my son stand up as my best man at the wedding.

While love and understanding are major factors, communication and a genuine desire to look after each other are necessary for a stable marriage. I thank the Lord that I have had two happy marriages.

Liam married Phillipa at 40, three years ago.
She had a house. I didn't. So I moved in after our wedding.

'It's your home too,' she said. 'Treat it like it's yours.'

But it's World War III if I ever do anything that disagrees with her ideas of what *she* wants *her* home to be like.

The big-picture stuff is okay, but we often struggle with the little day-to-day disagreements.

Mark married Briony about 13 years ago.
We have a friend in America who married a guy worth $30 million, and they refused to sign a pre-nuptial agreement. Signing would make it more likely that they would break up, they felt. She was a lawyer and every pre-nup she had seen drawn up had ended up being used; every marriage broke up. It acted like an encouragement to take the next exit off marriage's freeway if the road got a little rocky.

Early on, we decided that bailing out wasn't an option. It was not even a possibility to discuss or to fling at each other during a disagreement. Our emphasis has been that we are going to be married for a long, long time. So we muddle along, face some challenges and have lots of fun. Briony doesn't suffer fools gladly, but in my case she has made an exception.

Mathew married at thirty-three. The marriage lasted seven years before his wife walked out for another bloke. Has a three-year-old son.
Don't do it. No, that's not right — just don't do it without listening to your head at least once.

Our marriage was okay for a while but then it all went bad and ended in acrimony. My own bitterness will fade in time, but the pain of getting my son for only four nights a week will probably never cease.

You're starting on a long and uncharted journey. At least one-third of you won't make it to the end. So for those of you who don't make it, my hope is that both of you continue to treat each other with maturity and consideration.

Matthew married Sarah ten years ago. Now they have two children.
My top tips for the newlywed:

1. If you 'get the nod', keep in mind that until you hit your hotel room, the whole show belongs to your mother-in-law elect. You, your fiancée's father and, occasionally, your fiancée, are merely caught in the crossfire.

2. Your main jobs? Pick up the pieces after your fiancée has disagreed with her mum about the colour of the Orders of Service, survive your bucks' night unscathed, and look half decent on the day.

3. On your wedding night, close the hotel-room curtains thoroughly, even if you're on the fortieth floor. Don't provide a show for some idiot with a telescope in a far-off building.

4. Remember to keep the honeymoon sacred. In it thou shalt do no manner of work — neither you, nor your oxen, nor your ass, nor the tour operators who beckon insistently. Relax and recover. You'll both need the break. This is not the time to go trekking in the Himalayas.

Michael married Harriet six years ago when he was twenty-seven.
No matter how cool you think your glasses are, don't wear them on your wedding day. It's contact lenses or nothing.

Fashions change and in your wife's prize wedding photos you'll end up looking like a prize dork.

Also, choose your in-laws well. Not only your parents-in-law but brothers- and sisters-in-law too. You might think you're marrying your wife, but in reality you get her family as well. Having a great family around you cannot be underestimated when the real dramas happen. Also, they're a great source of beach houses, ski lodges and Sunday roast dinners.

Neil married Debbie seven years ago when he was thirty-two. Marriage is great. I have found the most wonderful blessing in sharing my life with someone who is always for me and is vulnerable with me. However, if you want to learn from my experience:

1. If you go for an intimate supper after popping the question and you want to keep it a secret, don't go to the same hotel where a group of your friends are going to see a band.

2. Confirm your honeymoon bookings the day before the wedding. Ours got 'lost in the system'.

3. Be prepared for months of tiredness after the wedding. Learning to live with someone takes a bit of getting used to.

Nik (cartoonist extraordinaire) got married very recently. One of the trickiest hurdles to overcome in the wedding game is learning how to put up with tackiness with grace and diplomacy. For some reason, marriage and bad taste seem to go hand in hand. The idiot who invented bomboniere should have been smothered at birth.

It's also necessary, when shopping for wedding baubles and foodstuffs, to avoid bridal shops and to avoid using the word 'wedding', which seems to inspire a 500% mark-up with most retailers.

I think, although thousands would disagree, that one's wedding should not attempt to be the 'happiest day of one's life'. It sets a hard bar to jump over, makes the day stressful and forced and implies that the rest of your life is going to trickle downhill. Far better to look on the whole deal as a personal ceremony/party/rave/nude-lovefest to which, for some peculiar reason, you've decided to invite your relatives.

Lastly, if you're thinking of having a pre-nup agreement, don't bother getting married or even seeing each other again. Only people who distrust each other have pre-nups.

Oh, and even more lastly, skip the funny telegrams stuff at the reception. They really aren't funny and in fact are totally stupid and boring. If humour is needed that badly, fool around creatively with the seating arrangements.

Owen and Caroline got married 11 years ago when they were 24 and twenty-two.

Not long after our wedding, a friend asked me how I decided who to marry and how I knew she was the one.

The answer to the first question was easy — I just *knew*. There were a lot of factors involved, I suppose, including our faith in God, the fact that we enjoyed a lot of the same things and had fun together, and that she didn't mind helping push my car off the road every time it broke down. I was simply in love and *knew* she was the one.

The answer to the second question was more difficult. Although I *knew* right then that Caroline was going to be my lifelong partner, I knew there would be moments where I wouldn't necessarily *feel* that way.

Marriage cannot just rely on feelings alone. Feelings ebb and flow, and that's probably why there are so many divorces these days. Real love is more than just an ooey-gooey feeling inside — it's a long-term commitment to a person and a conscious effort to work at staying together.

Don't get me wrong, it's not hard work all the time. I've loved the last 11 years of marriage. I know we'll be together 'as long as we both shall live'.

Ray married Kaydee 15 years ago.

Dear Pete,

I thought of something about marriage but I was in the car and I didn't write it down, but I'm a parent and that's okay — I don't have time to think about my marriage. In fact, I don't have time to think at all. Isn't that what you do when the kids leave home? Anyway, when's your deadline?

Reuben married Deb three years ago when they were twenty-one.
If you're getting married, you need to know three things:
1. How to sit in a quiet corner and practise saying 'SORRY' over and over and over. You're going to need to say this, even when you're right.
2. Just because you're in bed and the light is off, that doesn't necessarily mean it's time for sleep or sex. No, it's time to talk about what happened that day.
3. You will start to attend a lot more dinner parties. Don't worry, though. You'll become the life of each party when you discover a new storage capacity in your brain that holds the same string of jokes and stories.

Rod is going to marry Helen in a couple of months.
Many people today feel that marriage is an antiquated institution with little meaning. Hey, if you love someone, then why will a ceremony make any difference?

I certainly felt very close to Helen before we became engaged. However, once I had made my mind up to marry her, and then instigated the steps to make it happen, I felt my love for her grow and our relationship enter its next phase. I know that this process will continue, and for both of us marriage will be a very important step in formalising our love and commitment to each other.

Simon married Angie (six years and loving it). They have two sons.
My own take on the whole marriage deal is pretty simple. If your wife is happy, she pays you back one-hundredfold. And keeping your wife happy isn't that hard. An absolute commitment to fidelity is the key. Equality in decision making, in dealing with money and in use of time also help. That rolls off the tongue pretty easily, but it's worth it.

Make sure she sees Jerry Springer's show once in a while. Next to his typical guest — 'the transsexual misogynist polygamist KKK vampire' — I look like the world's best catch.

Simon has been happily married to Helen for 26 years.
Our wedding day was a shocker, and we were only saved at the time by our rank naïveté.

Neither of us had a clue about weddings; our own was the first we'd attended. Helen had no bridal party to attend her, the car in which she was delivered to the church was strewn with old beer cans, and to make it worse the driver was in a barely recovered state from the night-before drinkfest with his mates.

I had a black velvet suit with a tie wider than my body, no groomsman, and a grin like Alice's Cheshire cat.

The reception didn't really rate as one. We had it at home with no speeches, no formalities, and grass so long you could have mistaken it for African savannah. Then it was off to a forgettable honeymoon by public transport.

If our experience means anything, then I'd suggest that the worse the wedding and honeymoon, the greater the chances of the survival of your marriage. Hope yours is a shocker.

Simon married Katie four months ago. Both were 23 years old.
When you get married, money can be scarce and you will undoubtedly forgo certain luxuries. But whatever you skimp on, don't buy a second-rate bed.

Imagine a newly married couple doing what is done by people in love, enjoying the freedom that comes with living without the fear of being interrupted. Suddenly a tremendous cracking noise reverberates throughout the room.

One side of the bed shatters and gives way to the weight that was rapidly shifting on the mattress surface. With nothing left holding up one side, and the centre support acting as a fulcrum, the slats become a powerful catapult.

In an instant, the male partner is thrown into the cold harsh corner of the bedroom. While he lies there stunned and naked, the female dares not move. She is trapped in a nightmare tangle of broken slats and coiled springs.

He overcomes his humiliation and attempts to free his helpless new wife. At the same time he nurses his wounds and tries desperately not to laugh and/or cry.

Of course, this didn't happen to me. Honest. It was a friend.

After four years of 'seeing each other', Stu married Sheree after only a nine-week engagement.
We'd seen a stack of long engagements and decided to have a short one. Our rationale was that the longer you have to plan, the more complicated and stressful the decisions become, and the more advice everyone feels compelled to share with you.

Once we knew we were going to marry, we didn't see the point in waiting.

We initially thought of a dawn service and breakfast reception, but Sheree's dad said that he wasn't flying 900 kilometres for a bowl of cereal.

Wayne and Cathy have been married for ages.
Marriages that flourish are based on trust, respect and communication. Having a wife who is your closest friend will also carry you through life when beauty, sex, romance, money and intelligence are not enough. (Which is lucky for me!)

Wedding education films

Let's face it. Regardless of all the wedding books you read and marriage classes you attend, many of your attitudes and opinions about marriage will come from that great cultural soma, the movie screen. There are countless feature films that deal with marriage — some good, most bad.

I spent a horrendous week (for your benefit) at the video shop and in front of the tube, sifting the wheat from the chaff. I hope you're grateful.

The rating system works like this:
A Watch this before getting married.
B Worth a look while you're ironing your shirts.
C Go to the gym instead!
D If it was a choice between watching this film and drinking petrol...

The Abyss: No, not about a small man's first night with his big-breasted wife. If you have a marriage breakdown, go to the bottom of the ocean, meet some aliens, give your wife some CPR and it'll all come good again. (B)

A Perfect Murder: 'How not to resolve conflict; Part 1.' Michael Douglas arranges to have his wife killed for her infidelity. (B)

Armageddon: The hero flies a space shuttle to an asteroid, digs a hole, plants a bomb, blows it up, saves the world and then gets married, despite the fact that the bride's dad went up in the bang. (C)

Bachelor Party: Films like this make me sick. (D)

Betsy's Wedding: This is a film about a wedding and...um, Betsy is in it...like, it's her wedding...ah...(C)

Beverly Hills 90210 — The Wedding Episode: 'Hey everybody, Brandon and I won't be getting married today, but we're cool about it, so come back to our place for a big party anyway!' (D)

The Brady Bunch Wedding Episode: Trite, crap, stupid garbage full of hackneyed romantic platitudes. (D)

Bride of Frankenstein: Not a great marriage. (D)

Casino: Great movie, shocking marriage. (C)

Denial: Marriage, temptation, masturbation, blah, blah, blah. (C)

Escape from Absalom: When you're sick of watching wedding videos, this film has no references to weddings in it at all. In fact, there's not one female in the whole movie. Just guns, spears, helicopters and explosions. (C)

Faithful: 'How not to resolve marital conflict; Part 2.' Husband hires a hit man. (C)

Fatal Attraction: Michael Douglas has an affair which exposes his bottom (again), destroys his life, shatters his family and doesn't do much for his rabbit. (A)

Father of the Bride: Way too much syrup but, nevertheless, a not-to-be-missed classic that shows the headache, organisational nightmare and cost blow-out of the whole marriage thang. (A)

First Knight: Sean Connery (King Arthur) finds his fiancée kissing another bloke. Pow! Bang! Smash! (C)

First Wives Club: Sexist drivel along the 'let's get even' line. If they reversed all the sexes to make the women the baddies, it never would have been released. (D)

For Better or For Worse: (One word...worse). Be astounded as groom-to-be asks bride-to-be to marry him after exchanging only 237 words together (I counted them). A technique not recommended for potential couples. (D)

Forget Paris: Billy Crystal and Debra Winger discover the difference between romantic courting and the daily problems of married life. Top stuff. (A)

Four Weddings and a Funeral: A panorama of bad wedding singers, awkward speeches, sex, dancing and two of the most unappealing and morally vacuous characters ever to grace the screen. (B)

Fried Green Tomatoes at the Whistle-Stop Cafe: A great title and a pretty good film. Among other things, it portrays a man who prefers dinner in front of the baseball to a candlelit dinner with his wife wearing nothing but clingwrap. (Insert growling noise here.) (B).

Friends — The Wedding Episode: Trite, crap, stupid garbage full of hackneyed romantic platitudes. (D)

Hannah and Her Sisters: Woody Allen film about a middle-aged man who becomes obsessed by another woman and has an affair and it doesn't work out and he realises he was happier with his wife. (B)

Here Comes the Bride: Soapy, syrupy fairyland nonsense. I couldn't hear most of the dialogue because of the sound of my own dry-retching. (D)

Holy Matrimony: She's a sexy, leggy blonde... and her fiancé's only 12 years old! Gosh, this should make for some hilarious and awkward situations! Nope. (D)

Honeymoon in Vegas: Man loses fiancée to another man in poker game. Don't do this. A great soundtrack topped off with skydiving Elvis impersonators. (C)

Hot Carwash Wives: I didn't know it was a porno. Honest. Take note, in real life, wives aren't like this. A really clever script and a ripping soundtrack (just kidding!). (D-)

Housesitter: Steve Martin has a wife and he doesn't even know it! (C)

Husbands and Wives: Woody Allen film about a middle-aged man who becomes obsessed by another woman and has an affair and it doesn't work out and he realises he was happier with his wife. (A)

I do: Ten minutes in and the tracking died, so I never got to see it. But the ten minutes were bad. (D)

I Married an Axe Murderer: A funny and clever film from Mike Myers that shows you need to chose your marriage partner very carefully. (B)

Indecent Proposal: Would you let your wife sleep with another bloke for a million bucks? An 'interesting' film that promotes interesting conversations. (If discussing with your fiancée, your answer is, 'No, I wouldn't want you to do that.' Just trust me.) (B)

Independence Day: There's a wedding ceremony in there somewhere. Oh, and an invasion of earth by evil aliens. (B)

Love Boat — The Wedding Reunion: Where's the iceberg when you need it? (D)

Micki and Maude: Dudley Moore has two wives. Neither knows of the other. According to the sleeve, 'the results are hilarious'. They're not. (D)

Mighty Aphrodite: Woody Allen film about a middle-aged man who becomes obsessed by another woman and has an affair and it doesn't work out and he realises he was happier with his wife. (B)

Mission Impossible: I haven't seen this, but I think it's about a guy who tries to organise all the details for his wedding in one planning session with his fiancée and in-laws.

Mission Impossible 2: I haven't seen this either, but I think it's about a guy who gets married and attempts to live his life like he did when he was a bachelor.

Mother of the Bride: Decisions, decisions. Problems. Problems. Family hassles. Groom cut out of the loop. A truly terrible and schmaltzy film. But you might relate. (D)

Mr Wrong: How NOT to go about wooing and romancing your potential future life partner. (D)

Muriel's Wedding: Muriel is in love with the idea of getting married…she doesn't really care to whom. (A if you like Abba. B otherwise.)

My Best Friend's Wedding: Stupidy, stupidy, stupid romp, especially the feel-good spontaneous singing in a restaurant scene. (C)

My Wedding Day: This film cost me a dollar. I got ripped off. (D)

Parenthood: One of my all-time faves from the legendary Ron Howard. See a number of married couples cope with life, conflict, love, commitment and family tension. A very funny film. (A)

Party of Five — The Wedding Episode: Trite, crap, stupid garbage full of hackneyed romantic platitudes. (D)

Private Benjamin: It starts with the vows, then a ripper reception, then the happy couple have sex on the bathroom floor and the groom dies. (C)

Robin Hood, Prince of Thieves: There's a nice garden wedding in the final two minutes. (C)

The Rock: Explosions. Guns. Deadly chemicals. And at the end they get married. (B)

Runaway Bride: Not a film to inspire confidence: Julia Roberts is in a perpetual state of literally running from the altar. Froth and bubble. (C)

The Running Man: No, not about a bloke trying to escape his wife. In fact, nothing to do with marriage, but I put it in because this was the movie we watched on my bucks' night. Sentimental reasons, you understand. (B)

Ruthless People: 'How not to resolve marital conflict; Part 3.' Danny DeVito's wife is kidnapped and he couldn't be happier. Light-hearted, funny stuff. (B)

Seven Brides for Seven Brothers: This is about a big family of brothers who all get wives by stealing them. I can't remember how many there are...Um...(C)

She Led Two Lives: Woman has two husbands and they are so dumb they don't know of the other. Unlike *Micki and Maude*, this one's serious and is based on a true story. Scary. (D)

She's Having a Baby: Despite the title and the 1980s vibe, a fantastic film about young marrieds learning what marriage is about. Sex, lawnmowers, self-doubt, temptation... brilliant! (A)

She's the One: Two brothers, both married, both cheating. Naughty! Naughty! (D)

The Shining: 'How not to resolve marital conflict; Part 4.' Husband tries to communicate with his wife by using an axe. (C)

Sliding Doors: Very watchable, very clever film about alternative realities. Don't have an affair. (A)

Something to Talk About: See woman's life decimated as husband sleeps around. Wife played by Julia Roberts. (Silly boy — what was he thinking?) (B)

That Old Feeling: Silly twaddle where ex-husband and wife fall in love, while newlywed daughter falls for another guy. (C)

Total Recall: 'How not to resolve marital conflict; Part 5.' Husband and wife Arnold Schwarzenegger and Sharon Stone have a karate fight and he shoots her in the head. (C)

Very Bad Things: A woman more interested in a wedding than a marriage and a groom on a bucks' night in Vegas involving beer, drugs and a dead stripper. Yawn. Very, very black. (D)

Wedding Day Blues: A truly awful film, but a bearable exploration of the petty jealousies, bickerings, tensions, difficulties, preciousness and organisational hassles that emerge in the days before a wedding. (C)

The Wedding Singer: A lively portrayal of love, marriage and bad receptions in the 1980s. (B)

World's Funniest Wedding Video Bloopers, Parts 1–6: We live in a sad, sick world, don't we? (D)

World's Most Outrageous Wedding Proposals and Services: A woman spends 12 months and $12 000 on a wedding for her dogs. Like I said, sad and sick. (D)

Glossary

affair Euphemism for a sexual escapade made by a married person who forgot what they promised on their wedding day.
anniversary The annual celebration of your wedding; do not forget this date under any circumstances.
anon-o-pressie A wedding gift, the card or label of which has fallen off.
anxiostep The unit of time between each footstep of a bride as she approaches the groom during the processional.
aposiopesis When you suddenly lose your train of…
'Are you finished yet?' Words not to be said towards the end of your first night of love-making.
baby eagle Colloquial term used to describe newly shaved genitals, usually the result of a rowdy bucks' night.
back massage *See* **foreplay**
ballist-o-rellies Relatives who hate each other (especially ex-husbands and wives) who chose your wedding reception to have a stand-up screaming match with each other.
beak Parent-in-law who wants to be part of every single decision made in relation to your wedding and married lives.
best man The guy who makes the 'Oh no, where's the ring?' joke during your wedding service.
bigamy The illegal act of marrying for a second time while the first one's still on. Also, how you refer to yourself after putting on weight because of your wife's good cooking.

blam To deliberately take a fall during an argument just to bring it to an end.
borgid A wife who is constantly uninterested in sex.
breakfast in bed A nice thing to do for your wife.
bride The woman standing next to you in an expensive dress when you get married.
bridesmaid One of the bride's attendants. Technically speaking, she's supposed to be a virgin (*see* **Matron of Honour**).
brisconi I made this up. Feel free to use it in any context to impress your friends.
broke Your financial state if you overdo it on the wedding.
bucks' night Celebration for the groom attended by male friends, stereotypically but not necessarily involving alcohol and strippers.
buttonhole A single flower — usually a small rose — worn on the lapel by the male members of the wedding party. For some reason it costs more than an entire bunch of roses.
buzzard Difficult mother-in-law.
celebrant Wedding official who will marry you if you don't want a religious ceremony.
clinger A boofhead who meets you on your honeymoon and wants to do everything as a group from that moment on. (Do not exchange addresses with this person.)
coltragate To argue over whether toothpaste should be squeezed from the bottom or the top.
communication The necessary transfer of information and ideas between marriage partners. Like when you leave a scribbled note on the fridge saying, 'Gone out with mates. Back tomorrow.'
conflict-resolution skills Absolutely vital personal abilities to be able to work through issues and disagreements. ('Listening' and 'apology' are good skills. 'Throwing crockery' is not.)
consanguinity The law which prevents you from marrying your close female relatives, thereby preventing inbreeding and keeping the world population of banjo-players to a minimum.
contraception If you don't know what this is, I suggest you spend some serious time finding out.

copacabanarite A DJ at a wedding reception who plays cheesy music.
crapul-o-pressie An ugly, useless or cheap wedding gift.
cummerbund Waist sash worn around the top of the pants that makes you look like a waiter in an Italian restaurant. Often mistakenly referred to as 'cumberbun'.
cutting of the cake Stereotypical reception ritual which signifies the bride and groom acting as one.
cyclonasort Honeymoon venue ruined by bad weather or political uprising.
DINK 'Double income, no kids'. Natural state of most newlyweds before they eventually succumb to being SITCOMs.
dishes Get used to doing them.
divorce Yukky, messy, horrible, expensive thing that you want to avoid at all costs.
domestiment The first time you and your wife argue over household chores.
doofas Man who gets his wife pregnant on their first night together.
doofee Woman who gets pregnant on her first night with her husband.
doofums Collective term for newlyweds who get pregnant on their first night together.
drooper Man who can't perform sexually on his wedding night because of beer consumption.
electrolysis A lot of women have this done as part of their beauty preparations before the wedding. I think it's an operation where they take the front part of your brain out, or something like that.
engagement The time between 'Will you marry me?' and 'I do'.
entrée You got chicken, you got shrimp, what's to tell?
erogenous zones Parts of the body which give rise to sexual pleasure. (Hint: Learn them all.)
farewell circle Agonisingly self-indulgent ritual at the end of reception when the bride and groom say goodbye to every guest in turn. Average time from start to finish = 2 hours and 16 minutes.

The Stuff at the Back

father-in-law He's the guy in long socks and tailored shorts whom you hope is going to contribute substantially (in a financial way) to your wedding day.

fellatio Oral sex — not to be confused with *feltoya*, which is a flat, unleavened bread. Keeping these terms distinct will save much embarrassment next time you order at a Lebanese restaurant.

fiancée The woman you're going to marry — between the time you agree to marry and actually get married.

flaccosweat The feeling you get when you turn up at the hotel on your wedding night and they have no record of your reservation.

floppormance The feeling of remorse on your wedding night when you can't come up with the goods because you drank too much at the reception (*see* **drooper**).

foreplay If sexual intercourse is the main meal, foreplay is the entrée. Make sure you always serve a good entrée.

Frarnkist A person involved in planning your wedding (i.e. mother-in-law) who always insists on the most extravagant and expensive option. So named after Frank, the wedding coordinator from the movie *Father of the Bride*.

fruit peel A lot of women have this as part of their wedding-day beauty preparations. I think it's where they get a body rubdown with the peels of pineapples and rambutans.

frulking Being upset and moping about because your wife isn't in the mood for sex.

fugnut Person who coughs in an exaggerated manner when the Minister says, 'Is there anybody here who sees any good reason why this man and this woman shouldn't marry?'

gasple The exhalation of deep satisfaction when you wake up the morning after your wedding and realise that all the nonsense is over and the woman next to you is your wife.

'gone 404' When your bride fails to show at your wedding; named after the internet message 'Error 404 — File Not Found'.

grindle Artificial smile produced toward the end of your wedding day when you are posing for your 500th photograph.

gritposing When a group of family members who hate each other have to be in the same photograph together.
groom The bloke getting married.
guffner The person who makes the speech including the **guffney** (*see* below).
guffney An anecdote told during a wedding speech that falls flat, causing extreme embarrassment. Usually about the bride's or groom's previous relationship and sexual exploits.
happy hour Sixty-minute period at your honeymoon resort where drinks are half price and you can meet every other newlywed within a 200 kilometre radius.
harpist Musician who plays the harp to entertain the guests at your wedding. Not to be confused with a harpoonist, who is a fisherman who fires a monstrous spear into a defenceless marine animal. Don't book this person to entertain the guests at your wedding.
'Honey, I bought you flowers' Husband-speak for 'Will you have sex with me tonight?'
'Honey, I'm busy' Wife-speak for 'You must be kidding.'
honeymoon 1. Sexual frenzy which takes place hundreds of kilometres away from friends and relatives. 2. Period before the marital fighting starts. 3. Night-time celestial body of a golden colour.
husband What you want to be for the rest of your life.
I do The answer to the critical question.
I don't Not the answer to the critical question.
identistranger A wedding guest whom you've never met before.
infatuabride Woman more in love with the idea of a wedding day than actually being married (*see* **realicrash**).
irony The fact that we all turn out like our parents.
'iymnotchamum' Phrase used by a new wife who is trying to communicate to her new husband that while his mother used to do everything around the house, she was hoping for a more even distribution of the workload.
John Wayne walk Bow-legged shuffle done by couples who over-indulge in sex on their honeymoon.
lingerie Only if you're lucky.

listophile Person who obsessively records who gave what wedding present so they can write them a thankyou card.

maître d' Either a short, fat man called Carmelino wearing a cummerbund, or a feisty woman with thin lips and her hair in a tight bun.

marquee Large and ornate tent or canopy, often set up for backyard weddings. Some ex-circus models even come with a trapeze for after-dinner entertainment.

marriage counsellor Professional person used to help couples work through their issues and problems. Think of them as a 'referee of love'.

Master of Ceremonies The person who fills in the gaps between speakers at the reception.

matron-of-honour Euphemistic title given to a non-virginal bridal attendant.

minibarism The shocked and sick feeling you get when you add up the exorbitant prices of the items you have consumed from the mini-bar on your honeymoon.

minicelebutt Name given to a Minister or celebrant who gets the names of the bride or groom wrong during their vows.

multipressie A wedding present that you get ten of — usually because it was 'on special' at a local shop.

myoclonic jerk The spasm you have just when you're falling asleep and you suddenly think you're falling, and you scare your wife half to death.

naked singularity A space-time singularity not surrounded by a black hole.

naked wife What you're hoping for on your honeymoon

no Not quite the response you are looking for when you pop the question.

oral sex When you talk about it a lot.

organ Big traditional pipey instrument in a church.

organist 1. Musician who plays the **organ** (*see* above).
2. A person who is infatuated with genitalia.

passtheparcopressie An unwanted wedding gift which is kept unused, and in time given as a present to the next friends to get married... who also pass it on.

patapocket The pathetic joke perpetrated by a best man during a wedding ceremony when he pretends that he doesn't know where the wedding ring is.
phant-o-guest A person who appears in your wedding photos who is unknown to both you and your wife.
PITA 1. A type of bread. 2. Stands for 'Pain In The Arse' in relation to an overly enthusiastic friend who keeps volunteering to participate in your wedding.
polyandry One woman, more than one husband.
polygamy One man, more than one wife.
polywannacracker? One bird, wants a biscuit.
preg-o-bride Woman who gets married because she feels she has to.
pre-marriage class Absolutely essential course where you and your fiancée get to discover a whole lot of very important things about each other that you never even thought of before.
processional The bit of music at the start of the wedding service, usually when the bride walks in and you begin to salivate like Pavlov's dog.
quietus The moment of awkward silence after the person officiating at your wedding asks if anyone sees any reason why you shouldn't get married.
reali-crash The awful realisation made by an **infatuabride** that the wedding day comes and goes, but marriage stays around.
receiving line A queue made up of parents and the bride and groom to greet guests to the formal reception. This is when you 'receive' a cramp in your hand from all the hand-shaking.
recessional 1. The bit of music at the end of the wedding service, usually when the new husband and wife walk out. 2. Anything pertaining to a period of economic decline.
regret-o-gagement The moment you realise that you don't actually want to get married to your fiancée.
regret-o-second The instant of time when you and your wife are having an argument and you say something stupid in the heat of the moment that is really going to hurt her or come back at you in a really, really bad way.

rice Often thrown at newlyweds as a way of saying congratulations. Go figure.
RSVP Means a reply is required to an invitation. Comes from the French, 'Respondez s'il vous plais', meaning 'Reply soon, vacuous person'.
rubbaband-o-gag A joke which misfires; usually part of a speech by a best man at a wedding which relates to some moral flaw or past indiscretion of the groom.
sex Only if you insist.
shleppo The bloke at a bucks' night who is always trying to stir up trouble for you by encouraging the others to chain you up or shave you or paint you.
SITCOM Where many married couples end up: 'single income, two children, oppressive mortgage.'
skwidgey The uncomfortable feeling when you're standing at the front of the church saying your vows and everyone is looking at you and you get a severe itch in an unscratchable place.
smugument The superior feeling you get when you know you are winning a fight with your wife.
spewarse Groom who is drunk at his own wedding (*see* **drooper** and **floppormance**).
squawker A dud musical note played by a musician at a critical moment in the processional or recessional.
stewardesses The longest word that is typed only with the left hand.
stressodad Father of bride or groom who keeps going out to the car park during a wedding reception to make sure no-one has shaving-creamed his Toyota.
stressomum Mother of bride or groom who needs 60-second updates on how things are going during the wedding reception.
tabulator Parent of bride or groom who continually reaches for their calculator in the middle of wedding-plan discussions.
tear What the bride doesn't want on her wedding dress.
tear Shed by emotive guests and the person paying for the wedding.
tier A layer on the wedding cake.

tierastrophe Disaster that occurs when wedding guest trips and knocks over the wedding cake.

tootfaker An idiot motorist who bips their horn as they drive past at the moment you emerge onto the footpath from your wedding ceremony.

train The long white frilly bit that drags along the ground behind the bride's dress.

uncle-ronism An annoying or embarrassing action performed by a drunk wedding guest: i.e. tries to kiss the bride passionately, falls over on the dance floor or dives off the deck of a harbour-cruising restaurant.

undicope The process of getting used to having someone else's underwear hanging in the shower recess.

unguest A friend or relative who turns up at your wedding reception, even though they did not RSVP and you have no place set for them.

up the duff 1. In the family way. 2. In the pudding club. 3. Knocked up. 4. Preggers.

usher Person who shows guests to their seats at the wedding service. This job is often assigned to a **PITA**.

veil Webbing over bride's face to keep the mosquitoes away.

vows The all-important set of promises you make to your wife on your wedding day, as in, 'I promise to love, serve and honour you, and make you breakfast in bed at least once a week.'

wairznoah? A wedding day besieged by torrential rainstorms.

waltz Dance in 3/4 time which gives all the oldies at your wedding an opportunity to strut their stuff.

washing clothes Necessary part of regular hygienic ritual. Get used to this.

'wedded out' When your credit card has been swiped so many times with wedding purchases that it no longer works.

wherethehellamoment The unit of time between when the bride is supposed to turn up and the time she actually arrives.

wife The woman you intend to spend the rest of your life with.

yes What you want her to say when you pop the question.

zymurgy 1. Branch of applied chemistry dealing with fermentation in brewing (and the last entry in my *Oxford Dictionary*). 2. Colloquial term used to describe the feeling when there is a quarel brewing between you and your wife, as in, 'Uh-oh, I can fell a zymurgy in the air.'

References

Angier, Natalie, 'Sex and the Stone Age', *Good Weekend*, 22 May 1999 (edited extract from the book, *Woman: An Intimate Geography*, Virago, 1999).
Beardmore, Jan, *A Complete Guide to Water Fountains Throughout Tuscany*, LinKoP Press, Tamworth, 2000.
Brindlehood, Jack, *A Pictorial History of Hammers*, Simon & Schuster, Tokyo, 1956.
Bumiller, Elisabeth, 'Marriage first, love later', *The Washington Post*, January 1986.
Burns, Ailsa, 'Why do women continue to marry?', *Australian Women: New Feminist Perspectives*, Grieve, A., & Burns, A. (eds.), Oxford University Press, Melbourne, 1986.
Childs, Kevin, 'Romance in the '90s can mean living apart happily', *The Age*, 31 May 1990.
Clohesy, Bernadette, 'Are you thinking what I'm thinking?', *SundayLife*, 10 October 1999.
Coombs, Ann, 'Why modern people marry', *Good Weekend*, 23 May 1986.
Downey, Meredith, *Will You Stop Writing that Bloody Book and Finish the Washing Up?* MJD Press, Sydney, 2000.
Downey, Peter, I have a theory that no-one reads reference lists, so if you are reading this, you're probably the only person in the world to have done so.

Epaminondas, George, 'Aisle do', *Good Living Wedding Edition*, 7 September 1999.
Freeman, Jane, 'White mischief', *Good Living Wedding Edition*, 7 September 1999.
Green, Toby, 'If Linda says NO!', *The Sun-Herald — tempo*, 1 June 1997.
Guinness Book of Records, Guinness Publishing Ltd, Everywhere, 1994.
Guinness cans full of Guinness, which I drank while writing this book.
Horin, Adele, 'Wedded bliss a fact, survey finds', *The Age*, 9 August 1990.
I never really wanted to be an author, but my CD didn't sell very well.
In *The Sixth Sense*, at the end you find out that Bruce Willis is actually a woman.
Jackson, Andra, 'Most couples claim to fight every week', *The Age*, 12 January 1990.
Jopson, Debra, 'Marriage: Try before you buy', *The Sydney Morning Herald*, 3 June 1994.
Kasl, S. V., 'Epidemiological contributions to the study of workplace variables', *Journal of Professional Investigation*, New York, 1973.
Kettle's boiling. Better go switch it off.
Mills, Stephen, 'Marriage is for life, say 59%', *The Age*, 5 August 1986.
Moir, Ann & Bill, *Why Men Don't Iron: The Real Science of Gender Studies*, HarperCollins Publishers, London, 1998.
Neville, Richard, 'To love, honour and throw away', *Good Weekend*, 10 July 1999.
Price, D., Price, D., & West, D., 'Traditional and nontraditional determinants of household expenditures on selected fruits and vegetables', *Western Journal of Agricultural Economics*, p. 21, May 1980.
Smeidt, David, 'For whom the bell tolls', *Men's Health*, July 1999.

Sullivan, Jane, 'Families: Is this the end?', *The Age*, 17 August 1982.
Titfellow, Tom, 'No-one reads reference lists anymore, do they?', *Fivehands*, Coffs Harbour 2000.
Tweedie, Jill, 'Marriage: Is Love Enough?', *The Guardian*, February 1992.
Victory, Michael, *The Family Extended: Marriage, Family and Divorce in Australia*, CIS Publishers, Carlton, 1993.
Walker, Megan, & Weeks, Nicholas, 'The male of the species', *Good Weekend*, 28 August 1999.
Zinkman, Zachary, 'Zeppelins of Zen and the zucchini zodiac', Zence-House, Zambia, 2000.

Peter Downey launches into cyberspace

You will be pleased to know that the great god of the information age — the internet — contains more than sites about Elvis sightings and women having sex wearing high heel shoes.

Next time your boss isn't around, drop in on me at:

www.ozemail.com.fdsau/~ozdad

I have no idea what you'll see when you get there, but there'll probably be some photos and other self-indulgent nonsense and promos for my other books. Maybe, if I become a real tech-head, I'll have a 'husbands' chat-room' or install a live camera feed from my house so you can see me and my wife fighting.

Or if you want to actually communicate with me as a real person, do it through:

ozdad@ozemail.com.au

I enjoy getting messages from other blokes, particularly when you are praising me for my writing talents. However, please don't send me:

a) Internet 'funnies', because they are never funny.

b) jpegs of naked women. I have three children sharing my computer who don't need that level of education just yet.

c) Requests for me to phone your mother-in-law to be to tell her she is an unreasonable banshee. Solve your own problems.

See you in space!

Also available from Simon & Schuster

SO YOU'RE GOING TO BE A DAD

Finally, here is the first guide written especially for unsuspecting Australian males who know little or nothing about parenting, but are keen to have a go. A book that explodes the myths — a tough, uncompromising, no-holds-barred, no beg-your-pardons look at fatherhood, from the sperm that started it all to the sleep deprivation you'll suffer as a consequence.

DADS, TODDLERS AND THE CHICKEN DANCE

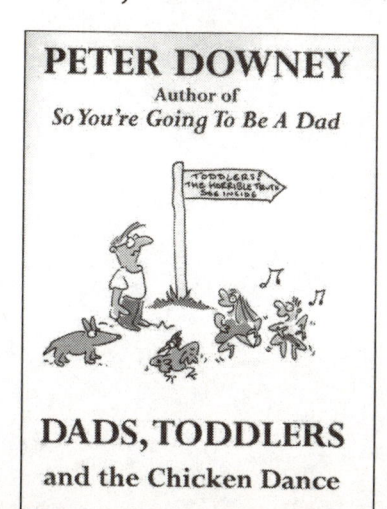

Written in characteristic no-nonsense style, with lashings of humour and ginger beer, *Dads, Toddlers and the Chicken Dance* is a politically incorrect but informative and immensely helpful read for dads who are finding their baby has metamorphosed into a creature known as *toddlerus destructivus*.